THE TRANSACTIONAL
ANALYST IN ACTION

THE TRANSACTIONAL ANALYST IN ACTION

Clinical Seminars

Michele Novellino

Routledge
Taylor & Francis Group

LONDON AND NEW YORK

First published in English 2012 by
Karnac Books Ltd.

First published in Italian in 2010 as *Seminari clinici. La cassetta degli attrezzi
dell'analista transazionale*

Published 2018 by Routledge
2 Park Square, Milton Park, Abingdon, Oxon OX14 4RN
711 Third Avenue, New York, NY 10017, USA

Routledge is an imprint of the Taylor & Francis Group, an informa business

Translated by Andrew Brociner

British Library Cataloguing in Publication Data

A C.I.P. for this book is available from the British Library

ISBN 9781780490700 (pbk)

Edited, designed and produced by The Studio Publishing Services Ltd
www.publishingservicesuk.co.uk
e-mail: studio@publishingservicesuk.co.uk

CONTENTS

ACKNOWLEDGEMENTS

This book, like all books, must give due recognition to the many people who have, directly or indirectly, influenced it.

I remember, first of all, the man who introduced me to transactional analysis, Carlo Moiso, who, though he is no longer with us in body, remains spiritually present as being the first person in Italy to have believed in transactional analysis: thank you, Carlo, my first master and dear friend; I know that you would be proud to see that the seed you sowed, in me and in others, is flourishing.

Thanks to all of my other masters and sponsors, from Richard Erskine to Jacqui Schiff, and I am also grateful to many distinguished colleagues, from Jim Allen to Ulrike Mueller, who have supported my attempt, often solitary in difficult years, to fight for the recovery of the unconscious.

A special thank you to the *Transactional Analysis Journal*, especially as represented by Bill Cornell and Robin Fryer, for the attention that has always been given to my papers.

Infinite thanks to my many students, many of whom today direct important and well-known schools of training . . . I remember you all with affection and gratitude.

Thanks to Laura Bonanni . . . for making the metaphor of the lobster known to me.

Thanks to my patients, who continuously invite me, through their participation, to interrogate myself on the validity and the real effectiveness of the techniques about which I write: you are the only real check for what I practise and teach.

Michele Novellino, psychiatrist and psychologist, teaching and supervising transactional analyst (TSTA) of the International Transactional Analysis Association (ITAA) in psychotherapy and in counselling fields, is one of the founders of transactional analysis in Italy. He was granted the Eric Berne Memorial Award in 2003 for his studies on unconscious communication, and is the author of twenty books on psychotherapy and more than 150 papers.

William F. Cornell

In his volume of clinical seminars on the theory and techniques of contemporary transactional analysis, Michele Novellino accomplishes two things: he carries the reader into an in-depth elucidation of the psychoanalytic roots of the work of Eric Berne, and positions transactional analysis of today firmly within the framework of psychodynamic and relational models of psychotherapy and psychoanalysis. Novellino offers a thorough and profoundly respectful reconsideration of Eric Berne's clinical techniques, who has for far too long (since the publication of the runaway success of *Games People Play*) been dismissed as the originator of a "pop" psychology. In these pages, Berne emerges as a serious, psychoanalytically based theorist. Novellino's writing is dedicated to the recovery and elucidation of the psychoanalytic roots of Berne's work and to a fundamental understanding of unconscious dynamics at the heart of the therapeutic process.

For more than three decades Michele Novellino has been articulating a model of transactional analysis deeply rooted in an understanding of unconscious dynamics and the interplay of transference and countertransference dynamics, which had come to be somewhat obscured in Eric Berne's use of colloquial speech and terminology. His efforts were rewarded with reception of the Eric Berne Memorial Award in 2003. This volume of clinical seminars represents the synthesis of his efforts since the 1980s. The result is a book that will inform and reward not only transactional analysts, but all psychotherapists and counsellors involved in psychodynamic and relational approaches to personal growth and development.

The book opens with an overview of contemporary transactional analysis in its various theories and manifestations. For readers unfamiliar with transactional analysis, Novellino provides a current and comprehensive introduction to the state of the art (or science, if you prefer). For those familiar with transactional analysis, Novellino begins to introduce the theme of the centrality of unconscious communication that is elaborated throughout the subsequent pages. To some transactional analysts, his argument that there is an unconscious level of experience in the Adult ego state will challenge some of the more traditional, cognitively based viewpoints in transactional analysis.

Eric Berne distinguished himself from the psychoanalysts of his day by emphasising the therapist/analyst's responsibility to promote *change* as well as understanding in one's patients. In the second chapter, Novellino articulates the role of the therapist as an agent of change. In the opening chapters, we see a model based in the direct and active interaction between therapist and client and the establishment of a bi-personal field of mutual engagement and reflection.

It is in Chapters Five, Six, and Seven, discussing Berne's methodology and the use of the therapeutic setting and contracts, that I found the heart and soul of Novellino's book. In these three chapters he takes central concepts in the practice of transactional analysis and infuses them with new depth of meaning. He begins with a very early (and brief) article by Berne, "When is the patient really in therapy?", in which Berne characterises the patient's commitment to psychotherapy as the result of three "divorces": the Child ego state of the patient "divorces" his/her own internal Parent ego state, thereby forming an initial alliance with the therapist cast as a new parental figure, followed by another "divorce" from the Parent of the therapist, and, finally, from the Adult of the therapist in establishing autonomy and one's own self-reflective capacities. Novellino reminds us that ego states are not simply roles, but are enduring "states of experience" with elements of both conscious and unconscious structures and capacities.

In Chapter Five, Novellino differentiates the therapeutic tasks from the therapeutic *setting*. Here he makes what I see as a major innovation in TA theory and technique. Transactional analysis has long emphasised the importance of the therapeutic contract as a means of establishing the mutual engagement of patient and therapist in the work at hand. Novellino holds the tension between the more cognitive–behavioural elements of TA practice, that is, the avoidance of psychological games and the engagement of the Adult ego state, and the underlying psychodynamics of transference and countertransference and the interpretation of unconscious motivations and meanings.

Novellino elucidates the important distinction between the *content* of the therapeutic contract and the *process* of carrying out the contract. Novellino places new emphasis on the working environment, such that the treatment contract establishes not only the objectives, but also the frame and process of the work. Transactional analysis, in keeping with many psychoanalytic and relational models, has long recognised the importance of the therapeutic relationship as an essential object and means of change. Novellino stresses the *frame* of the working environment as equally important as an object of transferential projection and resistance as well as a mechanism for change.

It was in *Principles of Group Treatment* (1966) that Berne most fully elaborated his philosophy of treatment. Novellino provides us with a very careful review and elaboration of Berne's clinical thinking. In so doing, he offers us a conceptual and technical base for the therapist's ongoing clinical decision making. While Berne was known for his humorous and often irreverent style of writing, we are here brought to a reading of Berne as a very skilled and reflective clinician.

Transactional analysis has been a fundamentally interpersonal mode of psychotherapy, whether in individual or in group treatment. In the closing chapter of this book, Novellino takes the reader into more recent models of transactional analysis, with particular emphasis on the unconscious, *intrapsychic* dynamics points of impasse in the treatment process. Here, the focus shifts from the dynamics of person-to-person communications to the internal dynamics and communications (or lack thereof) among the patient's states of ego or within the memories, fantasies, and needs of the Child ego state.

Throughout these pages, Novellino sustains careful and systematic attention to the patterns of unconscious communication between patient and therapist. In so doing, he stresses the responsibility of the therapist's ongoing engagement in self-analysis. While Berne was clearly a thoughtful and responsible psychotherapist, his was what would now be considered a one-person model of psychotherapy. Berne's formal psychoanalytic training was in the ego psychology of the 1940s and 1950s (Paul Federn and Eric Erikson having been his analysts). Berne's transactional analysis was a psychology and psychotherapy of the ego in all its functions and manifestations. He was, perhaps, overly confident in the resources of the Adult ego state and the objective capacities of the therapist. While he did certainly acknowledge the risks and likelihood of therapists being inducted into patients' games, thereby becoming participants in the patients' scripts, there was little in Berne's writings about the therapist's subjectivity. While this book is deeply grounded in Berne's psychoanalytic roots, Novellino's model of a psychoanalytic transactional analysis brings new growth to the theory and techniques of contemporary transactional analysis, now newly rooted in the realms of unconscious processes and the nuances of intersubjectivity.

Introduction

This book was born out of the demands, which are more and more informed, for a manual that presents, in a didactic and systematic way, that which is considered "the toolbox" of a modern transactional analyst. In fact, since the publication in 1966 of Eric Berne's *Principles of Group Treatment*, it has not been possible to find a work that condenses the operative principles of the transactional method and shows how it has developed in a variety of methodological tendencies, although there are books on techniques related to single orientations.

In 1987, I published, with the editorial help of Achille Miglionico, a student at the time, a volume detailing the clinical seminars I had held until then in the training institutes of the IAT in Rome, Padua, Bologna, Naples, Palermo, and Bari. Although not commercially available, that "amateur" edition enjoyed surprising success. It was very quickly out of print, and continued to be circulated widely among the students of the Italian schools. Since that time, much water has flowed under the bridges of both transactional analysis and of my professional life. As a scientific community, we have grown from being enthusiastic pioneers in those early years of awareness of transactional analysis in Italy. This growth was initiated by my lamented friend and colleague Carlo Moiso, with whom I entered into a joint enterprise that at the time seemed almost impossible: that of making acceptable an approach that was seen as alternative in the academic and professional world, where the impregnable fortress of orthodox psychoanalysis had hardly even noticed the only psychotherapies that were considered "acceptable"—cognitivism and systemic therapy.

However, today there are dozens of recognised schools of transactional analysis, some very different to those affiliated with two of the associations that Carlo and I founded, the IAT and the AIAT.

Since 1987, then, two Eric Berne prizes have been awarded by the International Transactional Analysis Association, one for the work of Carlo Moiso on the ego states and transference (in 1987) and the other for my work on unconscious communication and interpretation (in 2003). That recovery of the psychoanalytic roots of the work of Berne, which led to international recognition of the Roman School of Psychodynamic Transactional Analysis, was a realisation of the dream that could be discerned in various articles published in the *Transactional Analysis Journal* in the 1980s, but that is now evident to all.

In the wake of the pragmatic philosophy that guided the work in 1987, transactional analysis has been reviewed and updated through the lessons that I give during the training seminars for transactional analysts and didactic transactional analysts at the Eric Berne Institute in Rome, and also at other schools of transactional analysis (Auximon and IRPIR of Rome, the Turin Institute of TA, the Centre of Dynamic Psychology of Padua, the Centre of Psychology and TA of Milan). The subject is also covered in other schools, such as the Institute for the Study of Psychotherapy and the Italian Society of Reichian Analysis of Rome.

The topics in this book are presented in such a way as to offer both students and psychotherapists an assimilable view of what the current panorama of transactional techniques offers, particularly in respect to those of a psychodynamic orientation, but also providing ample coverage of the re-decisional techniques. Less well-known techniques are illustrated, too, such as the intervention on the Parent, and others that are more recent.

The focus of the manual is on the technical aspects of the transactional analysis intervention, thus integrating previous works on the epistemology and the methodology (*The Clinical Approach to Transactional Analysis*, 1998), and on the psychoanalytic roots of the Bernean work (*Transactional Pychoanalysis*, 2004). From these two works, I have extrapolated topics that are valid for particular themes, especially with regard to the epistemology and the general methodology and psychodynamics.

The manual does not present themes of a strictly theoretical type, except when it is necessary to facilitate comprehension of the method or the technique that is being illustrated, and in any case the reader interested in knowing more about such themes will find the necessary references in the bibliography.

The philosophy of the didactic adopted in the text is that of contributing a training in *competence* that derives from an acquisition of *know how* (knowledge of the methodology), based on a *knowledge* (knowledge of the theory).

I distinguish the techniques based on two criteria. The first is that of the structural level, or of the ego state "target"; the second is that of the school of orientation.

I hope that the text, which represents the synthesis of more than thirty years of the study of transactional analysis, together with the dissemination of its theories and methods in teaching it, will be useful to students, to the directors and the professors of schools of transactional analysis, and also to therapists of other schools, in that it will give them an up-to-date and comprehensive idea of the current state of transactional analytic methodology.

It was fun to write it, and also emotional: I saw many faces again, I heard a hundred voices again, the seminars that I led transpire in the pages that I wrote, and I felt again the same emotions that I experienced decades ago.

Finally, let me say that I would have liked someone to have written this book so that I could have read it many years ago, but, of course, in that case, I would not have felt the urge to do it myself . . . Enjoy your reading.

CHAPTER ONE

General principles

The Lobster

"A long time ago, when the world had been recently created, a certain lobster decided that the Creator had made a mistake. So he made an appointment with Him to discuss the question. 'With all due respect' said the lobster, 'I would like to protest about the way you designed my shell. You see, no sooner do I get used to my outer covering than I have to abandon it for another uncomfortable one, and, above all, it's a waste of time.' To this the Creator replied: 'I understand, but do you realise that it is precisely the leaving of a covering that allows you to go forth and grow inside another one?' 'But I like myself the way I am,' said the lobster. 'You really decided that?' asked the Creator. 'Of course,' replied the lobster. 'Very good,' smiled the Creator, 'from now on, your shell won't change and you will continue to be as you are now.' 'Very kind of You,' said the lobster and he left. The lobster was very happy to be able to wear the same old shell, but day after day, that which at first was a light and comfortable protection started to become a cumbersome and uncomfortable one. In the end, he got to the point where he could not even breathe any more inside his old shell. So, with great effort, he returned to talk to the Creator.

'With all due respect,' whispered the lobster, 'contrary to what you had promised me, my shell has not remained the same. It tightens more and more.' 'Certainly not,' said the Creator, 'your shell might have become harder with the passage of time, but it remained the same size. You changed inside, inside of the shell.' The Creator continued: 'You see, everything changes continuously. No one remains the same. That is the way I created things. The most interesting possibility that you have is to be able to leave your old shell when you grow.' 'Ah . . . I understand!' said the lobster, 'but You have to admit that that is quite uncomfortable.' 'Yes,' replied the Creator, 'but remember . . . each change brings with it the possibility of discomfort . . . together with the great joy of discovering new aspects of yourself. But you can't have one without the other.' 'All of that is very wise,' said the lobster. 'If you allow me, I will tell you something more,' said the Creator. 'I pray you, do!' replied the lobster. 'Each time that you leave your old shell and decide to grow, you will construct a new strength inside of you. And in this strength, you will find a new capacity to love yourself and to love those who are near you, to love life itself. This is my plan for each one of you.'"

(Anonymous)

Didactic introduction

The making of a psychotherapist, in addition to his school of thought, is based on three interdependent levels that are constructed after he has completed his training:

- *awareness*, both of theory (the knowledge) and of methodology (the knowledge of how to put the knowledge into practice);
- *competence*, given by the integration between knowledge linked to practical know-how and the individual capacity to apply and use what is understood in a particular context;
- *ability* to acquire effectively, through practical training, mastery, and command.

A transactional analyst will be worthy of his title not merely through gaining a diploma, but when he is able to utilise Berne's theories and techniques to their fullest extent in his practice. He has to have:

- a thorough critical knowledge of the works of Berne and the principal exponents of the schools (classical, redecisional, reparenting, psychodynamic, integrative) on which the theory is founded;
- a well-assimilated culture of psychotherapy, understood in both the descriptive and the structural sense
- a real understanding of the theoretical base and of the principal techniques (Bernean operations, redecision techniques, transference and countertransference techniques)
- the competence to apply one's own knowledge selectively to the clinical situation (ability at the therapeutic level)
- adequate personal resources (intuition and empathy) to allow him to create constructive interpersonal contact.

Competence, therefore, is the result of several years of study, personal analysis, clinical experience, supervision, and continual updating. This, of course, takes far longer than the four years usually required (in Italy) to become qualified; indeed, qualification is merely the first step on a journey that will last for an entire professional lifetime.

The current schools of specialisation in psychotherapy have the important deontological task of providing their student psychotherapists with the foundations essential for practising a profession in which learning extends far beyond a university curriculum, particularly since that is often restricted by a culture which does not encompass the complex learning that is the art of psychotherapy.

Definition of transactional analysis

Transactional analysis is definable as:
1. A philosophy of the therapeutic relationship.
2. A theory of the development of the personality and an interpersonal psychology.
3. A system of therapeutic techniques aimed at optimising the effectiveness of the therapist.

From a philosophic point of view, transactional analysis is a movement of humanistic psychology (Maslow, Rogers, & Perls), which, therefore, rejects a strictly "medical" concept of recovery: the problem presented by the patient is approached above all as a starting point for the growth of the psychophysical potential of the human being (fundamentally, of his being "OK").

There are some principles which substantiate that which has just been said.

Philosophic principles:
- OK-ness
- contracting
- decisionality.

The first (which Harris has disseminated widely in his book *I'm OK, You're OK*, 1971), is the *philosophy of OK-ness*, understood as the openness of the person to growing and learning from the experiences he has had, both positive and negative.

The second philosophical principle is that of *contracting*: the therapeutic relation is based on a contract, aimed at actively involving the patient in his therapeutic process.

The third principle is that of *decisionality*: a person is a responsible being who makes "decisions", but one's life script is often based on infantile decisions that are auto-limiting. Concomitant with decisionality is "redecisionality": that which at one time was decided can be *re*-decided.

Schools of transactional analysis

Barnes (1977) provides criteria suitable for defining when a particular transactional analysis approach can be regarded as a "school".

- The existence of the *leadership* of a teaching and supervising transactional analyst (TSTA), or a transactional analyst working under the auspices of the International Transactional Analysis Association (ITAA) (or the European Association of Transactional Analysis (EATA)), whose abilities are recognised in the fields of both learning and research. Such a leader has strong technical ability, and his role as a guide is defined by his ability to recommend: (a) a different theoretical direction; (b) a method which goes beyond that indicated by Berne; (c) a clinical approach which is cited in the literature and applied by many practitioners; (d) new ideas about continuous growth which have a national and international influence.

● The existence of a *group modality*, consisting of: (a) a *group charac-ter*, which reflects the characteristics of the personality of the leader; (b) an *ethical* standard of behaviour considered suitable for the professional; (c) a *technical culture*. These three components represent the three ego states (Child, Parent, Adult) of the leader and how they influence the members of the group.

A further criterion is that of assigning to the leader the Eric Berne Memorial Award by the ITAA.

On the basis of the parameters mentioned above, the following schools are currently recognised:

- ● Classical Bernean School (Steiner, English, James)
- ● School of Redecisional Therapy (Goulding)
- ● School of Integrative Psychotherapy (Erskine)
- ● School of Psychodynamic Transactional Analysis (Novellino and Moiso)
- ● School of Relational Transactional Analysis (Hargaden and Sills).

Other significant and often innovative approaches do exist, of course (for example, constructivism, described by Allen and Allen (2000, 2005)), but many are essentially theoretical, and, at the present time, cannot present evidence of efficacy from a methodological point of view.

The common features of the different schools are the following:

---

1. A system of theoretical reference which explains the concepts of the ego states, transactions, games, and script.
2. A methodology of intervening with the patient, based on the contract and on the redecisional process, with the aim of helping the person to abandon his original script.

With this as a base, different experiences and perspectives can fit well, thanks to the versatility of the theoretical framework.

Initially, this evolved, with the aid of Gestalt therapy, from the *redecision therapy* of the Gouldings (1978, 1979), and subsequently from the *integrative psychotherapy* of Erskine and colleages (Erskine & Moursund, 1988; Erskine & Trautmann, 1996): these two approaches led to more attention being paid to phenomena that take place *in* patients on an emotional level. Following this, interest turned to phenomena of a mainly unconscious nature within the relationship between patient and therapist, already amply described in the psychoanalytic literature, through the concepts of transference and countertransference (e.g., Novellino and Moiso's *psychodynamic transactional analysis,* Novellino's *transactional psychoanalysis,* and Hargaden and Sills' *relational transactional analysis*).

From a clinical point of view, we can distinguish three different levels of transactional analysis intervention (Novellino, 1998):

1. A *reparative psychotherapy* or "focal" psychotherapy, in which the transactional analyst, through a "social control contract" (agreement to therapy aimed at resolving a specific problem), helps the patient to resolve his or her specific problems with tools which are mainly cognitive–behavioural; in other words, a decontamination.
2. A *reconstructive psychotherapy,* based on *script analysis,* built on "autonomy contracts" and achieved through reducing confusion.
3. An *analytic psychotherapy,* which has as its objective, particularly in regard to analysis undertaken by trainee psychotherapists, an awareness of one's own unconscious dynamics, with the aim of preventing their projection on to the patient.

For the sake of clarity, let us designate reconstructive psychotherapy and analytic psychotherapy simply as *analysis.*

---

1. Focal psychotherapy (reparative).
2. Analysis = a. reconstructive psychotherapy + b. didactic analysis.

New epistemological bases

This section aims to examine the central idea of transactional analysis as psychotherapy, following the methodological lines of its original Bernean roots.

In particular, it focuses primarily on the importance of the *clinical method*, rather than on the theory, because, in line with what is happening in the psychoanalytic world generally, it is the theory that attracts criticism.

Here, a brief historical digression might prove helpful in clarifying current methodological developments.

Stewart (1992) draws attention to two problems that are well known to everyone:

- a distorted public image of transactional analysis;
- the isolation of transactional analysis compared to the rest of the psychotherapeutic world, which has led to Bernean thought having minimal influence on the latter.

Campos (2003) illustrates the current situation of transactional analysis through the analogy of a tree whose roots are well planted, but whose branches seem to be diverging from the trunk, risking a sort of suffocation. He identifies in particular three branches that are at such risk:

- integrative psychotherapy (Erskine & Moursund, 1988);
- postmodern constructivism (Allen & Allen, 2000);
- the psychodynamic movement (Novellino, 1984a; Moiso, 1985; Hargaden & Sills, 2001).

The same author recognises that for too many years transactional analysis was presented, by leaders of its own school, as something that was a sort of "one-dish recipe", if not, indeed, a psychology of *self-help*, which is entirely at odds with Berne's thinking.

I consider, on the other hand, that the historical originality of the work of Berne situates itself, on the one hand, with ego psychology and, on the other, adheres steadfastly to the developments which led first to object relations theory and then to relational psychoanalysis: starting from a drive theory, it moves to an interpersonal motivational theory. Berne's work ended up at a sort of junction, at which each form of psychoanalysis found itself, comprising both an evolution in theoretical research and a methodology in crisis due to the lack of clinical evidence. This placing renders transactional analysis as a psychotherapy characterised by phenomenological research on the personality being clearly understood in the interpersonal sense.

The principal human motivation is not tied to sexual and aggressive drives, but to what Berne calls *recognition-hunger* (1964): there is an innate and primal need to receive stimuli from the environment, and this "hunger" exerts a fundamental influence on the various aspects of the child–parent interaction.

> Attachment is a primary need, not a secondary one as in Freud.

In essence, Berne's theoretical and methodological apparatus places the relational events at the centre of both a metapsychology of the ego and of an analytic methodology.

Its starting point from a clearly Freudian position, and the fact that it remains anchored in an interpretative type of strategy, mean that transactional analysis is a *neopsychoanalytic psychotherapy*.

The ultimate result that derives from all the foundations of Berne's work is that transactional analysis is situated within the modern psychoanalytic movement. From this stems the proposal that Bernean theory should be recognised as a real *transactional psychoanalysis* (Novellino, 1998).

This renaming takes its starting point from the works of Mitchell (1988), among others. Mitchell places Sullivan at the centre of current psychoanalytic tendencies, and, as a result of this, the theoretical and clinical supremacy of psychodynamic research is distanced from the Freudian concept of drives and entrusted instead to a "pure" object orientation. In interpersonal models, the relational mind is a complex apparatus which regulates its impulses with the aim of maintaining its object ties but, at the same time, distinguishing itself from them: we are confronted with a *dyadic mind* in which desires and needs are experienced as the primary context of relations. It is the significance attached to the latter which determines the main motivation of human behaviour.

The *relational movement* proposes surpassing the juxtaposition of the intrapsychic and the interpersonal, considering, at the same time, the psychodynamic phenomena within a relational matrix. The relations are not to be understood as merely putting into practice internal object relations, but as the result of a primary necessity of the mind: an auto-adjustment of an interpersonal character. The schools of ego psychology, of the psychology of the self, and of object relations have greatly contributed to this change in thinking.

I consider that the Bernean model fulfils the epistemological criteria described by Mitchell, and, therefore, I shall summarise. Berne starts from the Freudian model. From that, he accepts the assumptions tied to the two structural and identifiable topics in the concept of the ego states and the unconscious dynamics present in psychological games and in the psychological script. However, he builds on those roots in a revolutionary way, proposing, in an unequivocal manner, that the primary motivation for behaviour is the psychological necessity of *hunger for stimuli and for stroking* (1964). The intrapsychic and interpersonal levels are seen as two sides of the same coin. Internal dialogue and interpersonal communication are the reciprocal mirrors of the individual's activity within his interpersonal context. The old models of interpersonal relations influence the current ones in a reciprocal dynamism: what has taken place with the original parent figures explains, in part, the transactional idea of the *here-and-now*, but the latter, within the psychotherapeutic relationship, leads to a continued elaboration of the former. The transactional vicissitudes are the results of a continuous interrelation between the past and the present; the Bernean mind is a dyadic type.

The real richness of psychoanalysis, beyond the acuity of its theories, lies in looking at the details of the analytic situation (*clinical method*), or at the particular interpersonal environment which is organised with the objective of achieving therapeutic results. This does not mean that the theories are superfluous, but that, given the present near-unanimity that psychoanalysis and psychotherapy have been shown to be effective in a practical sense, disregarding the theories that tried to explain them, the research should explore the factors that play key roles in the therapeutic setting.

Once transactional analysis is situated in the present psychoanalytic movement, different consequences result, of a cultural, philosophical, theoretical, and applied nature.

In the present environment of the clinical recovery of psychoanalysis, which should be seen as a real cornerstone of transactional analysis, a systematic exploration of the operative methods becomes important as an independent area of study and research.

All of this calls for a definition of the *clinical method* in order to compare the different conceptual views and the various interpretations. With respect to this method of reference, the differing theoretical concepts would be debated and modified. If, on the one hand,

Berne's work gave guidance on different ways to provide a clinical setting for a group (1966), on the other hand, he did not write anything about the setting in individual therapy. Therefore, in this latter area, I think it is necessary to update the analytic–transactional epistemology in order to join in with the present state of revolution in the analytical world.

> A conceptualisation of the individual setting in transactional analysis should result in overcoming the confusion and the irrelevance that presently affect the theoretical debate (Novellino, 1998, 2004).

In this context, I will limit myself to recalling just two key concepts that characterise the psychodynamic approach of Berne's psychology, and which, therefore, represent the foundations of the psychodynamic methodology.

The first concept is that of *transference impasses* (Novellino, 1985b, 1987).

Mellor's theory on impasses (1980) proposes an interesting "structuralist" revision of the "functionalist" model of the Gouldings. The impasses are presented as three levels of evolution to which the child–parent conflict can be attached. Mellor's model allows the phenomenon of transference to fit with that both structurally and developmentally, so that we have three types of fixational transference: cognitive, affective, and somatic.

In their turn, the three types of transference impasses provide the transactional analyst who works from a psychodynamic point of view with a frame of reference in which to analyse both the clinical problem of the patient and the different transference and countertransference phenomena.

The second concept is that of *unconscious communication* (Novellino, 1990).

The psychological level of the transaction can precede a level that can be interpreted only from the associative sequences that are provided unconsciously by the patient to the therapist. The patient can communicate his own transferences experiences only in decodified form, through "stories" and dreams, which symbolise a profound and unacknowledged stage in the adult–parent relationship.

I consider that what is described applies particularly if we use transactional analysis in the setting of individual psychotherapy.

Working in an individual setting with transactional analysis means primarily defining the parameters within which one can effectively achieve a script analysis. In a group setting, the analysis of the psychological script of the patient is achieved through the analysis of psychological transactions and games which the patient expresses with the other members of the group, leading to what Berne calls the analysis of the *group imago* (1961).

> In an individual setting, we should seek the conditions suitable for facilitating the emergence and acknowledgement of the infantile experience that is the basis of the script, or of the transference.

Therefore, the setting, as in psychoanalysis and in psychotherapy with a psychoanalytic orientation, assumes an essential value in that it allows for explanations of transference phenomena and their analysis. For instance, in a classic clinical situation, the way in which the patient participates emotionally in the frequency of the sessions is revealing.

As examples, a borderline patient will express his anger towards the therapist for missing a session, or expects him to make up for the times he was late. A phobic patient will often ask to have less frequent meetings in the critical phases of the relationship.

We can assert that:

> in the context of an individual transactional analysis, the setting constitutes the principal parameter for script analysis.

as it permits an individualistic approach to the manoeuvres through which the patient attempts, unconsciously, to recreate with the therapist the conditions that had resulted in his impasses and contributed to the consequent construction of his script.

In the same way, the countertransference of the therapist becomes a necessary instrument to follow the emotional vicissitudes of the patient (Novellino, 1984a). The phenomena of concordant and complementary identification help the therapist to perceive what occurs in the unconscious of the patient.

Transference and countertransference are not only interesting concepts, but the pillars of the work of transactional analysis.

Through the analysis of the phenomena of transference and counter-transference, the transactional analyst can reap what emerges from the script as a transference neurosis in the therapeutic relationship. The contamination that the patient has suffered is projected on the therapist, who then acknowledges it, helping the Adult of the patient to become aware of it (decontamination), and the Child to choose new options (deconfusion).

The transactional analyst uses interpretation as a central therapeutic tool, along with others, as described by Berne (1966). Interpreting, in the psychoanalytic sense, does not, of course, aim to substitute the adult of the patient, but to guide him towards an insight into how and why he repeats his past script decisions in the present.

The historical evolution of interest in the relationship between transactional analysis and its psychoanalytic roots can be found in the annals of the ITAA journal, the *Transactional Analysis Journal* (*TAJ*). Significantly, whereas from 1971 to 1989 the articles that explicitly dealt with this subject numbered fewer than ten, from 1990 to the present, their number has more than tripled. The first articles that signalled a return to the psychoanalytic base of the Bernean theory are those of Haykin (1980), Moiso (1985), and Novellino (1984a, 1985, 1987).

A thorough investigation of the issues connected with the evolution of transference and countertransference themes can be found in my two books, *L'approccio clinico dell'analisi transazionale* (The Clinical Approach of Transactional Analysis) (1998) and *Psicoanalisi transazionale* (Transactional Psychoanalysis) (2004), so here I will refer only to those works which have clinical resonance.

Erskine (in Hargaden & Sills, 2003) points to working with unconscious processes of transference as a method of therapy of the Adult ego state. The transference can lead to an identification of the old disruptions to inner or interpersonal contact. These disruptions in the contact and their correlated imaginations and fantasies constitute the subtle dynamics of transference. Transference is a constant attempt on the part of the client to put into effect the reparation of fixated infantile experiences through the simultaneous repetition of both the old defences and of the evolutionary needs to maintain relationships. In his methodological approach to work on transference, Erskine under-lines the importance of the capacity of the therapist to tune in with the rhythms, the experience, and the needs of the client.

Hargaden and Sills (2003) focus particular attention on transfer-ence, and alert the transactional analysts to the necessity of distin-guishing between gratification of the transference request and the real growth of the client: the former gives only a temporary relief. These two authors see deconfusion as a process through which the mental states of the child self can be brought to consciousness in the thera-peutic relationship. They write:

> . . . we consider all types of transference as an unconscious attempt by the patient to co-create a series of transactions that involve the thera-pist in finding the appropriate emotional and cognitive responses . . . every manifestation of transference contains both the potential for a transformation – the attempt to heal – and also the potential for the reinforcement of script. (p. 190)

On the whole, the term *unconscious* is used in the literature to mean two things:

- a neurophysiological process, important in the very first phases of development, leading to the development of the implicit memory system (Cornell, 1986; Gilbert, 2003; Gildebrand, 2003; Lee, 2003);
- in the Freudian dynamic sense, as to how it can be rediscovered in the process of transference and countertransference (Erskine, 2003; Gilbert, 2003; Hargaden & Sills, 2003; Moiso & Novellino, 1982; Shmukler, 2003).

Gilbert (in Hargaden & Sills, 2003) associates the Child ego state with the concept of representation of generalised interactions (RGI), defined as an abstract distillate of a certain number of specific memo-ries of the relationship of child–mother which share similar behav-iours: these can be re-experienced in the here-and-now. He also proposes a correlation between Stern's "imaginary friend" (2005) and the Bernean "parental influence".

Shmukler (in Hargaden & Sills, 2003) places transactional analysis in the present context of relational movements. She highlights how simple and clear language has damaged the image of the Bernean model, often causing it to descend to the level of popular psychology.

She also presents an interesting critical reflection on the future of transactional analysis:

> ... even if transactional analysis has much to offer as a thorough individual therapy, it also has limitations. The main one has to do with the unconscious processes: transactional analysis does not take them seriously enough; it offers neither a sufficient comprehension of them, nor a clear theoretical reference system within which to work with them. Many transactional analysts are not formed initially to work with transference. (p. 98)

Shmukler also talks about *relational developmental transactional analysis*, citing references to authors such as Moiso and Novellino (1982) and Hargaden and Sills (2003).

She also writes that

> ... when one wants to deepen the insight and the comprehension, listening to the unconscious messages becomes important. According to her, when we undertake an intensive and thorough long-term psychotherapy, it becomes impossible not to work with the unconscious dynamic and, as a therapist, one's own unconscious contribution to the relationship. (2003, p. 141)

She is one of the few authors to underline how neglecting the countertransference leads to processes of *acting-out*, with the consequent attention that is necessary to ensure that the environment furnishes adequate containment for the patient. In other words, she is the only one to state the question of setting.

Clarkson (1992) is one of the authors who contributed to the evaluation of the psychoanalytic roots of the Bernean opera. We will explore her classification of transference and countertransference in Chapter Nine.

Clarkson cites herself and Moiso and Novellino (p. 162) as the transactional analysts who actively work on transference.

Woods and Woods (1999) underline the usefulness of transactional analysis in the analysis of dreams and to the comprehension of desires and needs repressed from their Child ego state, defined by them as natural, with respect to Bernean terminology.

They propose a Freudian type of interpretative method, stating that "the Freudian theory of dreams and the analytical transactional theory of the Ego are more compatible than I had suspected" (p. 190).

Social, psychological, and unconscious communication

We start this section, which is taken in an edited form from "Transactional Psychoanalysis" (Novellino, 2004), with the study of what Berne had to say about intuition (1977). Berne dwells, in particular, on the concept of the *latent answer*.

In clinical practice, the latent answer refers to the communication of the subconscious reactions of the patient to his situation, and to the subconscious perception of these reactions on the part of the analyst, ideally without any interference from his own anxiety. In other words, in this situation, this refers above all to the perception of the transference reaction, with minimal interference from countertransference or anxiety. The latent answer could be represented by a preconscious flux of associations in the mind of the recipient (Berne, 1977).

In his theory of transactions (1961), Berne highlights both the profound point of contact with the psychoanalytic theory and progressing beyond that.

The type of transaction from which phenomena that are mainly of a transference nature emanates is the crossed one. Through this, these phenomena can be diagnosed at an inductive level.

In the *transference transaction*, the therapist sends a stimulus from his own Adult to the Adult of the patient (for example, "What is the reason for your being late?"), while the patient, experiencing the question as a type of parental reproach, reacts from his Child to the Parent of the therapist ("Why is he always so strict with me?").

In his later works, Berne abandons the psychoanalytic thoroughness of the transference and countertransference transactions to address the "theory of the social contact". In doing so, he underlines the motivational aspect of the transaction, understood as an event enacted to assure an exchange of stimuli between the sender and the recipient. If Bernean theory gains as social psychiatry, however, it forgoes the clinical thoroughness of the therapist–client relationship.

In 1964, Berne, referring to the three rules of communication, establishes that they are independent of the nature and of the contents of the examined transaction, but they refer exclusively to the direction of the vectors. Berne appears to ignore, therefore, the influence that other factors can have on the success of the communication.

The transactional analysis literature has not yet conducted an in-depth analysis of the transactions of transference with a psychodynamic base, within a Bernean framework of the rules of communication.

Unconscious communication (Novellino, 2003b) consists of a psychological message sent from the patient to the therapist, characterised as follows:

1.	The psychological level is unconscious, that is to say, inaccessible to the conscious by an act of will.
2.	The message is conveyed within a narrative centred on facts, events, and people external to the therapeutic relationship.
3.	The defences used are symbolisation and displacement.
4.	The psychological level of the message expresses itself not at the non-verbal level, as in psychological games, but, rather, through the unconscious construction of associative connections.
5.	The aim of the message conveyed at a psychological level is not something to benefit the script, but the expression to the therapist of an emotional content unacceptable to the consciousness.

The following is an example.

A young patient, during the initial phase of his therapy sessions, spoke of a recent situation with his father, who was worried about his performance at university, and, without consulting him, enrolled him in a private remedial institute. When he learnt about this from his mother, he felt very angry and was tempted to abandon everything. The therapist, perceiving at an intuitive level that the story in some way dealt with his relationship with the patient, suggested to the young patient that he think about the possibility that he himself was trying to say something implicitly. The patient, thinking about and discussing this, realised that something similar was taking place in the nascent therapy, in that it was being paid for by his father, and that, therefore, in the story he told, he was expressing his fear that, as a consequence of the financial aspect, his father might control him.

In the initial narration, the patient displaces a transference experience on an external event, in which appear figures that symbolise the therapeutic relationship.

In the light of the theory of unconscious communication, I have identified two classes of transactions, both interesting in connection with the analysis of transactional transference (2002, 2003b):

- *monologic transactions*, characterised by messages derived from a secondary process which acts at a conscious and pre-conscious level; these correspond to the first, second, and third types of transactions, and to the related rules. The transactions subsequent to the monologic class are explained by Kahler (1978), who considers that the stated psychological level is not "hidden" at all, but, rather, consists of the social manifestation of inconsistencies between two levels, which can be observed by an attentive analyst in the non-verbal process;

- *bilogic transactions*, characterised by a social level guided by a secondary process, and by a psychological level resulting from the primary process. The psychological level conveys messages in code about the therapeutic relationship. They are a type of subsequent transactions, for example, psychological games, but they do not comply with the third rule of communication, as they do not lead to a game pay-off. They are neither angular transactions nor duplex transactions.

Their detection can be achieved through the intuitive ability of the therapist to decodify the message.

The unconscious message could be connected with the two dynamics. In the first case, the patient conveys emotional material derived from script protocol: it is a transference projection in the classic sense; in the second case, the patient conveys, still in coded form, an experience of the here-and-now of the therapeutic relationship, but which he cannot express because of his old defences. The script is prohibiting him from feeling and expressing something that occurs in the therapeutic reality. The following is a classic example.

A therapist has to cancel a session, neglecting to rearrange it. In the following session, the patient tells of an episode in which he became very angry with his boss because he was not listening to him. Here, the patient's anger is really related to the behaviour of the therapist, but has to be repressed and symbolised by using a defence designed to avoid entering into conflict with his parents.

We can distinguish, therefore, two types of unconscious communication.

Unconscious communication

Type I: the emergence of emotions tied to protocol.
Type II: the emergence of emotions tied to the here-and-now.

In the first (Type I), the patient conveys protocol material. The social level is between two Adults; the psychological level is between the Child of the patient and the Adult of the therapist.

In the second (Type II), the patient conveys emotional material related to the here-and-now. The social level is still between two Adults, but so is the psychological level, because it is current. I will clarify what I mean by this. The concept of *an unconscious level in the Adult ego state* (Novellino, 2003b) represents a substantial difference to that proposed by Berne (1971), who described the ego states only in terms of conscious phenomena. I think that this concept of Berne's is incomplete and would benefit from being reconsidered. It is my opinion that the conscious, pre-conscious, and unconscious levels proposed by Freud are present in all three ego states, and that the Adult ego state can assimilate data of the here-and-now with only partial awareness, because of the defences of both the patient and the therapist.

Berne's first three transactional analysis principles do not apply to unconscious communication: the first applies only to transactions conducted at the social level, the second does not deal with crossed transactions, while the aim of the third is not to confirm the script, but to successfully communicate something considered unacceptable, so that the psychological level is not between the Child of the patient and the Parent of the therapist. Therefore, I introduced a *fourth principle* (2002), which is expressed as:

> the result of an unconscious communication depends on the intuitive capacity of the therapist to de-codify the psychological level of the transference transaction.

The ulterior aim of Berne's transaction principles is to reinforce at a behavioural level the role of the therapist's script, which is of intra-therapeutic benefit. The aim of unconscious communication is to bring to the therapist's attention material that will prove useful to the therapy. The game weakens the alliance; unconscious communication wants to reinforce it.

The fourth principle, therefore, is applied specifically to the therapeutic relationship, in contrast to the three of Berne.

I presented earlier a clinical example of unconscious communication in which the patient conveys a message to the therapist about feelings connected with his experience in the here-and-now of the therapeutic relationship. Let us now consider a clinical example that illustrates another possible aim of unconscious communication, or, rather, that which describes in an analogical way to the therapist an experience related to protocol.

L is a forty-year-old woman, had been in therapy for about a year for problems connected to a histrionic personality: repressed aggression and somatic agitation, an active but frustrating sexual life, difficulty in maintaining stable relationships. A previous therapy had ended because of a sentimental attachment to the therapist.

The setting calls for two one-to-one meetings a week. In this phase, the patient misses a session, and leaves a message on the answering machine saying that she could not attend. In the next session, without mentioning the session that she missed, she began immediately to talk about an event which had occurred in the preceding days.

Patient (P): "I want to talk about an ugly situation . . . really ugly, which happened to me the day before yesterday at work . . . I have already talked to you about how difficult the relationship with my boss is . . . do you remember? . . ."

Therapist (T): "Continue, we might return to your question later."

P: "OK [with a disappointed tone] . . . well, you know how I am always diligent at work, and above all you know the boss, well . . . it happened that I really could not meet a deadline because of an emergency, and the boss, who is always very strict with me, did not miss the opportunity to take issue with the fact that I was late . . ."

T: "And how did you feel?"

P: [After a long silence] "I don't know . . . first of all, I think a little worried, a little scared . . ."

T: "What were you scared of?"

P: "Well, maybe a year ago I wouldn't have told you this, or even admitted it to myself, but I felt like a child—a child who could be reproached. It is true that I did not meet the deadline . . . and maybe I expected the boss to be more understanding, to be a boss who would let things go occasionally . . ."

T: "I suggest that you read your story in this way. Keep in mind that in the last session something happened, remember?"

P: "I don't remember what we talked about . . ."

T: "This is precisely what we are talking about. You seem to have forgotten that last time you did not keep your appointment, and it is odd that you have not mentioned this at all. I think it possible that for you, who always attends regularly or, if you cannot, you ask if you can rearrange the appointment, this missed session has remained inside. You forgot about it, but also you repressed your related experience. Do you follow me?"

P: Nods.

T: "I think, therefore, that your unconscious experience is communicating to me very clearly through the story of this episode, because, if you think about it, it is so similar: there is a boss . . ."

P. "I understand! It is sort of your role to make the rules, and you who can . . . reproach me . . ." [she stretches and breathes deeply].

T: "Good! Now, are you ready to take another step? We should ask why you did not feel free to talk to me openly."

P: "I am not only ready, but now I think that I really understand . . . it was my father that I could not talk to about my conflicts, about my fears . . . at least that is what I thought."

Recent directions in literature

Three branches of the recent literature should be mentioned: narrativism, research connected to neuroscience, and constructivism.

Narrativism

Allen and Allen (2000) write that

> Constructivism and constructivistic thinking has had a limited but growing influence in transactional analysis. These views highlight the present-centeredness of relationships, including therapeutic ones, and the cocreation in dialogue and social interaction of ego states, transaction, games, and scripts. (p. 190)

They further state (2005) that their objective is

> . . . to supplement and expand traditional transactional analysis by bringing into the foreground the social constructivistic element that

we believe has always been in the background – the idea that each of us constructs (in concert with others) how we see reality, the story of our lives, and our idea of what should happen to people like us in this world. Berne's script analysis was one of the earliest of the distinctive narrative therapies. (p. 13)

Neuroscience

Many authors, from Cornell onwards, tried to update transactional-analytic theory in the light of the most recent scientific developments. For further detail on this theoretical area, one can refer to the book *Psicoanalisi transazionale* (Transactional Psychoanalysis) (Novellino, 2004).

Constructivism

Lee (2003) writes that

> The thesis . . . is a Constructivist one that sees the Parent and Child, as well as Adult, being created or co-created anew each day . . . A central thesis of the Constructivist approach is that a person's view of reality is co-constructed anew each day in the narratives she uses to 'make sense of' the world . . . it implies that ego states are literally recon-structed each day . . . People generally agree that Parent and Child ego states relate to the person's past; Adult ego states, by contrast, belong to the present. But when we consider this in the light of the Con-structivistic analysis, the distinction falls down; it is obvious instead that Parent and Child and Adult ego states are all experienced in the present. (p. 73)

Tudor (2003) considers the ego states as a useful metaphor to understand the personality rather than reality; he takes up again, therefore, the work of Loria to reaffirm that a problem that exists with the ego states was their reification. In synthesis, the basic concepts that the transactional authors elaborate with a constructivist orientation are the following:

- the ego states are in continuous evolution;
- the Adult is present from birth.

CHAPTER TWO

Change in transactional analysis

The change

Eric Berne, as a doctor, was interested in the recovery of his patients; his pragmatism was a rebellion, in many ways justified, against what he saw as the stagnation of the orthodox psychoanalytic method.

Presently, we should record different changes in the theoretical-clinical panorama, which make a revision of views which are radically opposite inevitable.

- The turning of clinical themes of classical neurotic and psychotic problems to situations of the narcissistic and borderline types, not always clearly delineated, has, in the last decade of the past century, caused notable changes to the different psychotherapeutic methodologies, from the psychoanalytic one to the transactional-analytic one;

- the assessment of psychotherapy in the field of practice instead of in metapsychology has produced interesting occurrences of convergence and often of integration;

- the increasing requests for training on the part of medical doctors and psychologists has caused changes in the way that training is conducted, although not always clear and justified conceptually;

● the entry of the psychotherapist into public services has created and, unfortunately, rarely resolved problems with regard to the method, the setting, and often even to the theoretical basis.

The conclusion is that, during the past few years, transactional analysis has undergone an important maturation process. While much of the initial spirit and almost all of the language of Bernean theory has remained, the methodology has changed profoundly and the clinical areas of intervention have increased. A salient point in this process seems to be the significant number of studies and works in which it is suggested that there should be a return to the neopsychoanalytic roots of the Bernean technique, and that the training required for becoming a transactional analyst should be updated, with the inclusion of the personal therapy of the student, in which Italy is a forerunner.

In what follows in this chapter, rather than dwell on detailed theoretical and clinical description (which exists elsewhere in cited works), I will focus on those things which seem to be fixed points in this phase, considered crucial for the evolution of transactional analysis:

● the recovery of the unconscious;
● the experimental method applied to psychotherapy;
● the recovery of the unconscious in psychodynamic transactional analysis: method and methodology.

For a thorough and effective understanding of the applications of transactional analysis, it would be useful to explore the following concepts (Novellino, 1998):

● clinical method: the theory of psychotherapy based on the study of relational events which mark the therapeutic interaction;
● experimental method: the application of the principles of the experimental method to psychotherapy;
● methodology: general theory of the technique; the final aim is the recovery of autonomy. This provides four strategic phases (alliance, decontamination, de-confusion, re-learning);
● strategy: the phase of the methodology dedicated to primary objectives;
● tactic: a single technique (operation) useful for reaching the objective of a single strategic phase;
● therapeutic plan: the practical application of the methodological principles to a clinical case.

By therapeutic plan, I mean the general direction that the therapist follows in order to satisfy the therapeutic contract of the patient, or, rather, to make a change. The plan foresees that the problem will be resolved in an effective way when the patient has successfully reintegrated the cognitive–behavioural–emotional–somatic levels (Erskine, 1980). The objective of the plan at this point (Novellino, 2004) could be the resolution of conflicts connected to the symptomology of the patient (reparative psychotherapy) or a global restructuring of the personality (reconstructive psychotherapy and didactic analysis). In both cases, the objective will be constructed to achieve the individual's recovery of "autonomy", which Berne (1964) defines as the state in which the person is capable of awareness, spontaneity, and intimacy.

The recovery of autonomy calls for a progressive resolution of intrapsychic conflicts (impasses), which assume cognitive, affective, and somatic forms based on the time of development and duration (respectively, fourth–eighth year for cognitive impasses, second–fourth year for affective impasses, first year for somatic impasses).

The execution of the therapeutic plan provides for the following four *strategic phases*, not necessarily linear, each one of which is intended to achieve particular objectives for partial change through the application of particular "tactics" or therapeutic techniques. These phases, which will be taken up again in the chapters on methodology, comprise the following:

- the phase of *therapeutic alliance*: the analysis of the explicit modality of the neopsychic structure in the patient–therapist relationship leads to the establishment of a therapeutic "contract", which identifies the initial objectives of the work, while the analysis of exchanges at the transactional psychological level leads to the construction and reinforcement of a positive transference alliance between the neopsychic structures of the therapist and the archeopsychic ones of the patient;
- the *decontamination* phase: aimed at liberating the neopsychic structure of the patient from the active esteropsychic and archeopsychic residue, in such a way that the neopsychic structure functions in the subsequent phase through the " observing" ego of the therapist;

> Observing Ego: the state of the decontaminated ego adult capable of auto-observing the intrapsychic dynamics.

- the *deconfusion* phase: aimed at resolving, through possible diverse technical procedures with the objective of permitting a "re-decision", impasses between esteropyschic and archeopsychic structures, which are the result of psychological decisions which led to the construction of the psychological script of the patient;
- the *relearning* phase: the aim is to reinforce and sustain the re-decision of the patient.

I summarise the specific goals of the four strategic phases in Table 1.

During the entire therapeutic plan, the transactional analyst will pay attention to the "sphincter" (Berne, 1972) level, identifying at which sphincter (time of development) the problems of the patient began.

The therapist, to help the re-decision of the patient, will provide him with the so-called three P's (Crossman, 1966):

> 1. Permission: that transaction through which the therapist helps the patient's Child to relieve him from the Parent's script messages can be given at each of the three states of the ego.
> 2. Protection: all of the procedures through which the therapist provides the patient with the environment suitable for confronting the fear of "disobeying" his own Parent (unconditional acceptance, setting, availability).
> 3. Power: capability in the timing and in the congruity of the intervention.

Table 1. The goals of the four strategic phases.

Strategic phase	Focal objective
ALLIANCE	Contract at the social level: positive transference and countertransference at a psychological level
DECONTAMINATION	Social control: the observing ego for the subsequent deconfusion
DE-CONFUSION	Re-decision: a "friendly divorce" from the old Parent
RE-LEARNING	Verification of the goals; detachment from the therapist

They will follow, furthermore, the general precepts of the *experimental method* (Novellino, 1984b) confirming their diagnostic and strategic hypotheses according to the *feedback* given by the patient through his messages, both linguistic and corporeal.

The syndrome of effective psychotherapy

The application of the experimental method to psychotherapeutic work can allow the therapist to construct strategies and tactics which, presented as diagnostic and operative hypotheses, are proposed to the patient, who will then either validate them or not, thus allowing the therapist to devise and follow an effective therapeutic plan for that client.

The result of this is twofold: in the long term it can provide a guide for the therapist so that he can help the patient to fulfil his contracts; in the short term it allows the therapist to verify, through some well-defined clinical parameters, whether or not the work that has taken place up to that point has been effective, and, therefore, whether it is proceeding towards a therapeutic change.

The outcome of correctly executed interventions by the therapist is a therapy which leads to the fulfilment of the therapeutic contracts (objectives) and, in parallel, to greater autonomy of the patient, within a positive fundamental therapeutic alliance: we call this global process the *syndrome of effective psychotherapy* (Novellino, 1984b).

The experimental method applied to the psychotherapeutic situation provides for progression through a series of phases; this progress constitutes, session after session, the continuum which unifies the various operations carried out by the therapist. These *phases* are the following:

The phases of the experimental method:

data gathering;
hypotheses;
verification of the hypotheses;
intervention;
feedback.

The data gathering phase

This phase provides the fundamentals indispensable for effective work, whether considered both in its long-term effect (fulfilment of the therapeutic contract) or in the short term (for example: first interview, contract of the session). It is only by the gathering of data that the therapist can select the best operative methodology, based on the requests and demands of his client.

The gathering of data is based on the following three criteria:

- *Listening to the material.* The therapist will listen to both the social and the psychological content of the transactions of the client, taking into account, therefore, the rules of communication laid down by Berne (1964); he will consider the associations (significant sequences) offered to him unconsciously by the patient, which frequently provide very significant material, most importantly to understand the unconscious transference situation of the client (Novellino, 1998).
- *Observation of the client.* This leads to the noting of different non-verbal processes useful for focusing on the situation of the patient, such as: incongruence between verbal and non-verbal communication; the acting out of the patient of particular therapeutic significance (for example, in patients with marginal personality).
- *Self-analysis of countertransference.* The self-analysis will be based on the therapist's awareness of his own reactions, which could provide illuminating answers regarding situations that are blocking the therapist–patient relationship. These reactions will be considered on four levels (Novellino, 1984b):

- behavioural: drivers, psychological games, slips of tongue, acting out;
- cognitive: fantasy and dreams, internal dialogue;
- emotional: racket emotions;
- somatic: hypochondriac and psychosomatic symptoms.

The suitable state for such self-analysis is that of "free-fluctuating attention", introduced by Freud and taken up by Berne (1972). The therapist has, therefore, the elements necessary to proceed to the subsequent phase.

Hypotheses phase

On the basis of the data gathered, the therapist can formulate a diagnosis of the situation of the patient on two levels:

> (a) structural–intrapsychic: historical and phenomenological diagnosis of the ego states, diagnostic identification of the script, individualisation of defence mechanisms;
> (b) relational–functional: behavioural and social diagnosis of the ego states, recognition of the type of transactions and of stroking, games, and script sequence.

Hypotheses verification phase

After explaining the hypotheses, the therapist will gather new data on the these. This step is indispensable, from the point of view of both methodological correctness and of ethics, before undertaking therapeutic operations which will affect the economising psychic of the client.

Intervention phase

The therapeutic operation executed at this point is considered to be one of the elements of the experimental methodology that we are outlining, and so its correctness needs to be verified through the subsequent feedback provided by the client. The key point of this phase of the method is that:

> the intervention is a consequence of a hypothesis, and, as such, needs to be validated.

If the intervention receives negative feedback (unconfirmed), the hypothesis earlier in the process needs reformulation, together with a revision of the intervention carried out.

Feedback phase

Through feedback analysis, the therapist can infer whether the intervention was correct and the relative hypotheses were valid, and, therefore, if the therapy is proceeding in an effective way. The feedback material is evident at three levels:

(a) material supplied by the client;
(b) material supplied by the group, such as an increase in cohesion, in intimacy, in the use of the Adult, etc.;
(c) material from the countertransference of the therapist.

The feedback can be positive, and so validate the intervention, or negative, and, in consequence, not confirm it.

Positive feedback

The identifiable aspects that I have described as the "syndrome of effective psychotherapy" are the following:

1. An increase in autonomy, in the components described by Berne (1964) of awareness, spontaneity, and intimacy.
2. An increase in the material provided by the patient for analysis.
3. An increase in flexibility in adapting.
4. A decrease in, and/or disappearance of, the symptoms.

This syndrome is characterised by both immediate effects and later effects, with respect to the intervention.

As *immediate manifestations*, we recognise:

- a reinvoking of significant material previously regressed: fantasy, dreams, infantile memories;
- a clarification of symptoms;
- an indirect confirmation: for example, the patient remembers a moment in which the therapist was helpful in the past;
- a verbal confirmation, which should always be validated by the presence of other manifestations: a simple "yes" or a "no" provided by the patient are not in themselves confirmations or denials, since they can derive from an attitude of either compliance or rebellion.

In the *late manifestations*, we recognise:

- the persistence of significant material;
- a consistently maintained absence of symptoms;

- the spontaneous transition of contracts from the "soft" type to the "hard" type;
- an increased capacity to exercise options;
- greater correlation between logical thinking (A2) and intuition (A1);
- the firm closing of the "escape hatches" of the script;
- more time spent in "activity" and "intimacy".

The noting of both immediate and later manifestations allows the therapist to obtain validation for the intervention, and also to reinforce the therapeutic alliance.

Negative feedback

In negative feedback, we notice some of the following manifestations:

- the lack of emergence of significant material;
- the constant presence of intellectualisation (pastimes or psychological games of "psychiatrist" and of "archeology");
- the appearance of regressive phenomena;
- the incidence of verbal agreement in the presence of non-verbal manifestations of negation;
- the formation of a *pseudo-alliance* based on the roles of Rescuer–Victim or of Persecutor–Victim;
- the emergence of new symptoms;
- the lack of fulfilment of the therapy's contracts.

The patient who does not change

One of the things that can be frustrating for the therapist, but also more interesting from a methodological point of view, arises from a psychotherapy that is ineffective; in other words, a patient who does not change with respect to the therapeutic contract.

Woollams and Brown (1978) list the following causes for a resistance to change:

1. An error in the execution of the strategic phases.
2. A problem with the contract.
3. Ambivalence in the therapist.
4. A problem of the transference type.
5. Resistance to giving up environmental strokings.
6. Working at a mistaken level without confirmation.
7. Being subjected to a "don't exist" injunction.
8. Script messages which are hidden and seek to prevent change.
9. An underlying order within a message from the counter-script on which work is to be done.

An absence of therapeutic change implies that a revision of the strategic phases is needed, and so we should consider whether there is:

- a mistaken set-up of the alliance phase, due to an error in the contract, or in the validation of it, or perhaps in the establishment of a positive transference relationship of trust and/or empathy;
- a mistaken set-up and/or conclusion in the decontamination phase;
- a mistaken set-up and/or conclusion in the de-confusion phase;
- a mistaken set-up and/or conclusion in the relearning phase.

We shall now look in more detail at the possibilities in this regard.

Error in the alliance phase

This could be starting the therapy without a valid contract, for example, a *Parent contract*: "I should stop smoking", "I should get on better with my husband", "My wife would like me to be closer to her". Another example is the contracts of "NOT being and/or NOT doing something" ("I should be less impulsive", "I don't want to arrive late"). It must be remembered that the therapist has to reach an agreement with the Adult ego state of the patient, and, where the motivation does not seem clear, carry out an initial decontamination so that the therapy begins only if the patient recognises the objectives he will work towards and in which he has reason to believe.

There might be an error in beginning the therapy with a *script contract*. For instance, the patient indicates a wish for change that appears credible ("I want to succeed in a career"; "I want to gain a degree"). There are cases in which, if a good anamnesis is not established and sufficient historical analysis of the script is not done, one might find that those goals wished for in completely good faith were, in reality, designed to confirm a script: for example, of "without love" or "without joy". This frequently occurs in the manic–depressive structure (Novellino, 1991), where the patient unconsciously follows the child's decision to try to obtain the approval of a parent who will never give it because enough can never be done.

A further cause of a mistaken set-up can derive from a *setting* that is not correctly established: an insufficient number of sessions, a lack of clarity of the rules, for example.

There could be a mistaken construction of the *alliance transference* (*pseudo-alliance*); essentially we find ourselves with a therapist who, unaware, is inveigled into a game. We enter into a complex subject, which is fully mature but must take into account the personal analysis and a capacity to analyse one's own countertransference. For example, if the patient in the first session starts a transaction of this type: "Doctor, have you already had cases like mine?", it seems that in asking this he is sending an explicit message, which, at a social level, might appear to come from the Adult ego state, but which could mask a psychological message of the type "I will make you fail!", dictated by an unconscious hostility from the Child ego state. If the therapist answers: "But of course, don't worry, you are not as bad as you think", he will form a *pseudo-alliance* of the Rescuer–Victim type, based on his particular *psychological gimmick* (for example, a narcissistic compulsion to accept a challenge, maybe to demonstrate something to himself). In the type of situation described above, the therapist has ask himself what the reasons are for the question, which will lead to an exploration of the initial transference fantasy that the patient has about the therapeutic relationship.

Frequently, it can be a mistake in the clinical assessment, such as starting the therapy with a patient for whom psychotherapy is not suitable at that time (sometimes, for example, in acute depressive phases or in paranoid confusion, it is advisable first to try a psycho-pharmalogical treatment in order to activate the Adult); sometimes transactional analysis is not the best psychotherapeutic route, but possibly a systematic family therapy is more suitable or a behavioural approach on its own.

Another possible difficulty arises when family resistance to change is not correctly assessed, and this can be true, above all, in the case of three-handed contracts: for example, in the case of adolescents whose therapy is paid for by the parents, the expectations of the latter can easily go against the objectives of independence and autonomy for the child.

The final thing to consider is a very delicate one. Each one of us, at the end of the various assessments we need to undertake in order to make a decision to start psychotherapy, should (with the Adult ego state) ask himself: "Am I the right therapist for this person?"

We know how, in the privacy of our study, we can make assessments which are not strictly clinical: the economic type (ours is, and has to be, a job), the psychological (we should never forget our narcissistic aspect, which might lead us to accept, for example, challenges that are not very realistic), and the environmental (external influences which lead us to accept that patient). We should always remember that a therapy that begins on an ambiguous basis can only lead to frustration, not only for the patient (who is, of course, the priority), but also for ourselves.

Error in the decontamination phase

In this phase, the most common mistake that can cause a malfunctioning therapy is that of not verifying the effective consolidation of the borders of the Adult:

- in the case of a therapy based on a *social control contract*, this means that the efficacy of the decontamination in alleviating the symptoms has not been assessed;
- in the case of an *autonomy contract*, this implies moving into the next phase (deconfusion) with a high probability of meeting significant resistance.

Error in the deconfusion phase

The primary error in this phase comes from a *pseudo-redecision* taken by an over-adapted Child. This is typical in the hysterical structure, in which the person "mimes" an intention to change (Novellino, 1991).

Error in the relearning phase

This phase involves, in addition to verifying the stability of the change (through a *follow-up* exercise, or through verification sessions, or by progressively reducing the frequency of the sessions), the working out of the *transference separation*. The therapist might unconsciously under-value the reciprocal experiences connected with the separation, and could, therefore,

- prematurely interrupt the therapy;
- delay the end of the therapy through procrastination.

"Sloppiness"

The aim of this section is to integrate the philosophy and the model of intersubjective psychoanalysis (Stern, 2005) with the basic principles of transactional psychoanalysis, in particular, its aspect of unconscious communication.

This integration emphasises the mental framework that the trans-actional analyst should utilise to help the patient face the subject of change, which mainly involves reflection on the position which we, as therapists, have to maintain towards that complex and difficult thing which is the management of the therapeutic relationship, if we wish to work in a psychodynamic way. Therefore, it is necessary for us to consider "how" to be in session.

The intersubjective model

First, I shall define the term "intersubjective": it is to be understood as the capacity to share emotional experiences with another person; in other words, to empathise with another person. This consists of a sort of thought-reading, though not in a magical sense, which can be achieved through the interpretation of behaviours manifested in both verbal and non-verbal ways.

The nature of intersubjectivity could have a biological base, through the mirror neurons, which map the information that the child constructs through observing the actions of others, thus permitting him to participate in the mental life of another; this process can begin only after the child leaves the fusion phase, the point at which he perceives the existence of two minds.

Therefore, there could be a neurobiological system of "echo", which permits one to understand, through the observation of actions and of paraverbal communication, what another person is feeling.

Most of us are born with the capacity to participate in the subjective experience of another; thus, each child is born into an intersubjective matrix. There are exceptions, of course. In autism, for example, there seems to be an incapacity to read the mind of another, which results in a serious failure of intersubjectivity.

Stern (2005) talks about a real "primary need for intersubjectivity", understood as a psychobiological need (therefore, a drive or an instinct) for psychological intimacy in which to share subjective experiences that is as important as Freud's sexual drives, Bowlby's attachment motivation, and Berne's stroke hunger.

As a drive (or a motivational system), the need for intersubjectivity promotes both the formation and the cohesion of groups, as well as the progress of psychotherapy. In essence, this need regulates the balance between two dimensions equally essential for mental development and the maintenance of its equilibrium:

1.   Psychological solitude.
2.   Psychological belonging.

In the theory of attachment, these two are equivalent to poles of proximity–security and of distance–exploration.

It must be reaffirmed that intersubjectivity acts in the service of two fundamental areas:

1.   Subjective orientation in relationships and in groups (where we are obviously in the field of intersubjectivity).
2.   The establishment of the identity and the cohesion of the self, with regard to the intrapsychic dimension.

In the development of psychotherapy, the dynamic interaction between the subjective experience of the analyst and that of the patient constitutes the recognition of the particularity of the intersubjective approach. For some psychoanalysts, the therapeutic intersubjective relationship calls mainly for the participation of consciousness; for others, it can include unconscious material; for some, it has to be recognised in an explicit way; for others, it can be implicit (neither of the two people involved knows what the other knows). It can be unidirectional and asymmetric (that is, occurring only to one of the two) or bidirectional (emerging, for example, during interpretation).

From a clinical point of view, in any case, it requires an awareness of the subjective states, and calls for a high level of attention to the non-verbal processes.

It can also be imaginary: in projective identification, imagination allows one to know what is in the mind of another, in an entirely different way to projection, which is constructed on a mere fragment of truth.

From a historical point of view, intersubjectivity has permeated the psychoanalytic discourse as a sort of occult task as far as the topic of transference and countertransference is concerned, mostly thanks to Ferenczi; in past decades, real schools of intersubjectivity have developed: Atwood and Storolow, and Greenberg, Modell, and Ogden, for instance. Similarly, we can speak of similar schools: interactional, relational, of the psychology of the self.

All of these schools, with different, more or less profound nuances, have identified some tasks fundamental to intersubjectivity which do not involve the strictures of classical Freudian psychoanalysis.

Let us look in a synthetical way at a comparison between the classical Freudian, or orthodox, approach and the schools which deal with intersubjectivity (Table 2).

From a methodological point of view, in the intersubjective approach, the central psychoanalytic subject constitutes material that emerges during a session from the co-creative exchange of two intersubjectivities. An early consequence is the necessity to be attentive to

Table 2.   Differences between classical psychoanalysis and an intersubjective approach.

Classical approach		Intersubjective approach
Objective analyst ("third person")	(1)	Subjective analyst
Subjective reality of the patient determined intrapsychically from psychobiology (drives) and premature experience	(2)	Subjective reality of the patient "co-created" from the subjectivity of the patient and the analyst
Intrapsychic	(3)	Social
Drives = monopersonal psychology	(4)	Relationships = bipersonal psychology
Positivistic logic	(5)	Paradigm tied to the theory of complexity and to chaos

the here-and-now: the present has a more central role than the past, and any memories are considered to be experiences which are occurring now, as the content of a story. The process of a session is considered to be centre stage with respect to its contents; the analyst pays precise attention to micro-events (a sentence, a silence, a turn in speaking, a change in posture) which constitute the dynamics (*relational moves* and *present moments*) that make up the raw material of the therapeutic interaction, and which, even if lasting for only a few seconds, structure the so-called "intersubjective field".

Through these micro-events, the analyst and the patient co-create a story in which it is possible to resolve "now-moments": for example, a silence or a critically unstable relational phase.

In this epistemological and methodological framework, "sloppiness" becomes an important clinical implement for the tasks of intersubjectivity. This term refers to the fact that the analytical process during the session is largely spontaneous and, above all, unpredictable at the micro-temporal (*moment-to-moment*) level.

Psychotherapy is a "sloppy" process, or, rather, an approximate one that stems from the interaction of two subjects who work on co-creating worlds to share, a process which is largely spontaneous and unpredictable, as it proceeds through trial and error, necessitating repairs and revisions of the latter. Therefore, "sloppiness" refers to the approximation, the unpredictability, the disorder inherent in the advancement of therapeutic work, which is less linear and more complex than one would like.

On the other hand, the approximation constitutes a potential source of creativity, considering the elements of surprise and of indeterminacy as a characteristic of the intersubjective field.

The errors are an integral part of the intersubjective process and, therefore, analytic. The false steps are precious, as the way in which the breaks and the repairs of the errors are managed constitute an important expression of the way to be with another; the sequence break–repair provides an important learning experience, similar to that which occurs in the mother–child relationship. In the intersubjective approach, "sloppiness" is not seen as a failing or a fundamental problem, but, rather, as an inherent characteristic of the subjective interaction that allows for new possibilities in the therapeutic process. Although it cannot be clearly identified, "sloppiness" is the product of two minds that work together.

Even silence is considered to be a relational movement that creates an intersubjective context for the direction that the therapeutic co-creation will take: the two subjects together look for, discover, and share, the reciprocal intentions.

In essence, this is the equivalent in two-person psychology of the eruption of unconscious material in one-person psychology.

The approximation inherent in the creative process which leads to the co-creation of a productive intersubjective context does not signify technical superficiality: the setting constitutes even more of a strong point in the analytic stock. "Sloppiness" is potentially creative only if it develops within a firmly established framework, therefore working with the basic rules of the technique.

"Sloppiness" in transactional analysis

In our Bernean way of working, the idea of sloppiness—of approximation and unpredictability—helps, in my opinion, to promote a beneficial "mental attitude" on the part of the therapist, who accepts and attends to a "relational climate" in which to immerse himself and to "learn while doing", aware that the contractual method and that which is said should help in the "doing". Certainly, it will help him to keep firmly in mind the objectives desired and agreed on with the patient, while accepting that "learning" will be, by its nature, "sloppy".

To have profound emotional material emerge, to construct a substantial alliance rather than a superficial one, the transactional analyst sensitive to the intersubjective dynamic should see himself as a captain of a ship. The "ship" is the therapeutic alliance, which, as we know, is based both on a "valid" contract and on a transference bond that begins positively; the element on which the ship travels can be a lake, or a sea, or even an ocean, depending on the type of contract. It will be a lake in the case of a short therapy, which I have previously defined as "repairing"; it will be a sea in the case of a "reconstructive" therapy; it will be an ocean in the case of a "true" analysis. In each case, one should not confuse the ship with the element: the lake, the sea, and the ocean each has its own mechanism of operation. The unconscious and the defence mechanisms are expressed, through transference and countertransference, through psychological games, and in what is said, from an intersubjective point of view in a "sloppy" way, and it is the ship, guided by the therapist, that steers the therapy in the right direction. It would be exceedingly deceptive and even damaging to expect to bend the lake, the sea, and the ocean to the technical procedure, which must, instead, serve to maintain a navigation consistent with the initial aims.

In terms of proper transactional analysis, we have further confirmation of the third rule of communication: it is the psychological level that determines the success of that communication. The psychological level is important even with respect to the micro-events described in intersubjective psychology.

I consider that there are particular affinities of orientation between this approach and that of intersubjectivity, and this is no surprise, given that it is proposed to give transactional analysis a place in the current movement of relational psychoanalysis.

The transactional analyst who really wants to actively address unconscious phenomena should accept, to take up the earlier metaphor, "trimming his sails according to the wind", knowing that the technique at his disposal does not work on the lake, or on the sea, or on the ocean, but on the ship.

From the point of view of content, I find some things particularly stimulating for the theory of unconscious communication: I highlight them here, being aware that they should be developed.

When one speaks of a psychological level and, therefore, of a narration, one is actually confronting one of the possible dimensions of unconscious communication.

I consider that those occurrences intersubjective psychoanalysts call "micro-events" can enter into that dynamic that I define as "unconscious communication", amplifying and enriching it, emphasising the importance of what can feature as a "rhythm" of the narration: a silence, a pause, a hesitation to put into words can accompany and corroborate the hypothesis that "that" narration is not, for example, a "pastime", but, rather, the expression of the attempt, and the hard work, of the patient to "co-create" a story experienced and present in a particular therapeutic moment.

To understand, in his turn, the presence of this particular channel of communication, the therapist (the captain of the ship) should grasp, feel, these micro-events inside himself, together with that which produces them, the pauses, silences, and so on.

Only in this way can the therapeutic experience be constructive and effective, riding the wave of the mental functioning of two individuals who work and feel together.

CHAPTER THREE

Defence and resistance

General principles

I n constructing the "toolbox", I consider an adequate understanding of the unconscious mechanisms that are at the base of therapeutic resistance to be indispensable.

Berne gave much space to the importance that the understanding and the awareness of the modality of functioning of the unconscious should have for the transactional therapist (1961).

The aim of this chapter, therefore, is to provide a synthesis of what is essential to know from a clinical point of view, without any pretence of entering into the delicate and complex questions of the order of metapsychology, which is the exclusive domain of the psychoanalyst.

> By defence is understood the intrapsychic unconscious process through which a person protects himself from the emergence of material felt as dangerous for the conscious equilibrium and of a conflictual nature. The defences are, in other words, the strategies of the ego against anxiety.

In the literature, many defence mechanisms are described, even if often there is no agreement on which and how many there are, to the point where different names are often used for similar mechanisms.

A useful criteria for the classification of defence mechanisms is a developmental one, which subdivides the various mechanisms on the basis of the phase of the development of the person in which these begin to establish themselves (White & Gilliland, 1975).

From this point of view, defence mechanisms can be considered a stiffening of the personality in a modality of adaptation, which, in a certain developmental phase, is normal.

For example, it is normal and physiological that a child makes a projective identification at a certain age, but if he remains "fixated" in this phase, growing up, he finds himself functioning with a primitive defence modality; similarly, when an adult person regresses, he will take up again the defence mechanisms typical of the phase of development to which he has returned.

> As resistance we understand, from a clinical point of view, the emergence of defence mechanisms in a certain phase of the therapy. The presence of a resistance will block the emergence of unconscious material, because that is the function of the defence, and it will prevent the progress of the therapy. It is important to underline the relation between the concept of defence, the concept of resistance, and the concept of transference: we find ourselves in front of a relation of the circular type.

When a patient appeals to a defence, he tends to enter with the therapist in a relation of transference which corresponds to the phase in which that defence belongs: that way, for example, the patient will adopt a projective identification with the therapist, therefore, as a parent figure appropriate to that developmental phase. Naturally, the contrary will also be true: a transference of the patient to the therapist implies that the patient is behaving with the therapist in a defensive way, just as he did with the original parental figures.

What has just been said about transference is true in the same way for the countertransference of the therapist.

Historically, at the beginning, the attention was centred around the patient, on his defences, on his resistance, on his transference; later, gradually, the accent was placed also on phenomena of reflection that occur in the therapist, on his defences and counter-resistance, which are verified when the therapist, putting into action his defences, blocks the therapeutic process. And, therefore, we speak of *counter-transference*, that is, of how the therapist, putting into action unresolved problems with his own parental figures, creates, in practice, a *counter-resistance*.

Countertransference: all the emotional experience of the therapist toward the patient.
Counter-resistance: defence system put into action by the unconscious of the therapist as a consequence of a negative countertransference.

At this point, the therapist–patient relationship is seen as a dyad of persons who influence each other, even through their defence and transference mechanisms.

From this point of view, the task of the therapist is to become aware of how, faced with the material that the patient brings, he tends to act unconsciously, and, at the same time, to maintain an Adult who observes what occurs and makes some sense of what takes place.

Let us take, for example, that which occurs with a depressed patient. It is often the case that, at a certain point in the therapy, the therapist begins to feel tired and irritable with his patient, and tends to function as a "Negative Normative Parent". The essential position that is stimulated is "I'm OK, you're not OK", and, consequently, the therapist tends to want to liberate himself from the patient, while the position in which the patient tends to place himself is that of the "Negative Adapted Child".

This is a vital point: if the therapist maintains an observing Adult position and makes some sense of what takes place, the therapy will be successful, otherwise, that which is defined as a "pseudo-alliance" will be created.

A *pseudo-alliance* refers to a relationship which is created based on the complementary positions of the personae of a dramatic triangle: "Persecutor"–"Rescuer"–"Victim". This relationship can sometimes seem quite engaging.

At this point, the Adult should be able to be present, otherwise the therapist "acts" the relationship, becoming, for example, irritated, or, worse, detached in order to repress the irritation, and can easily put into play an *acting-out*, a phenomenon which occurs when the emergence of significant material, in some way experienced as dangerous, instead of being channelled through the Adult, is processed through the Child. The significance of an *acting-out* on the part of the therapist is that this can cause him to abandon, or make himself be abandoned by, the patient, without being at all aware of what he is doing and the way in which he is doing it.

Acting out: action to unload non-thought-out emotions, in both transference and in countertransference.

Let us look at some of the possible acting-outs of the therapist:

Acting-out of countertransference
- forgetting a session;
- arriving late;
- prolonging a session;
- making a mistake on the fee;
- forgetting an important piece of information and behaving consequently;
- talking to third parties and forgetting to refer them;
- committing a "Freudian slip".

One of the ways a therapist has to face and resolve a situation is to hypothesise that what is occurring (that is, being pushed into the position of "Negative Normative Parent") is similar to the internal process of the patient (complementary identification), which, in its turn, is stimulating a "Negative Adapted Child"; this permits one to understand what is happening in the patient.

In fact, what typically happens with depressed persons is that they try to project externally part of their internal conflict, and, therefore, do things in such a way that the therapist becomes a Persecutor, replicating the rejecting Parent that the patients had introjected.

The important thing is that the therapist becomes aware that he is experiencing emotions that have to do with the patient and, consequently, orientate his guidance of the therapy in a suitable direction.

The *sequence of the internal dialogue* (Kahler, 1978) and the possibility that those sequences are projected or introjected, explain the process from the point of view of transactional analysis.

Defence and the developmental point of view

From a developmental point of view, each phase of a libidinal investment corresponds to a particular type of defence. Table 3 summarises this.

In the *oral phase*, we have, as defence mechanisms, *splitting* and *denial*. In *splitting*, the child divides reality between two poles and then denies one of the two poles. *Denial*, therefore, is the child's annulment of one aspect of reality.

Projective identification is a mechanism in which a child projects a part of himself, usually "bad", on an external object, with which he then identifies. In *projection*, however, there is also a splitting, but only the split part is projected externally, without the need for the child to identify with the object. From this point of view, *projective identification* occurs earlier and, therefore, is more regressive than projection.

In the anal phase, we have *reactive formation*, which is the defence mechanism through which the person enacts a programme (such as thought, behaviour, or state of mind) that is antithetic to that which he really feels; for example, as a reaction to a strong feeling of anger

Table 3.   Correspondence of libidinal investment to a particular type of defence.

	Phase	Defence
Libidinal development	Oral phase 0–1.5 years	Splitting Identification (projective, introjective, intro-projective) Projection Denial Omnipotence
	Anal phase 1.5–3 years	Reactive formation Affective isolation Rationalisation
	Phallic phase (or Oedipal) 4–7 years	Conversion Displacement Condensation
	Latency phase 7–12 years	Sublimation Regression

towards someone, the patient behaves very nicely towards that person. Reactive formation is typical of the obsessive personality structure.

Affective isolation is a mechanism through which the person deals with affective content considered dangerous without feeling the emotional echo: for example, a good friend or a family member of our patient dies, but he does not feel any pain related to that event. *Rationalisation* is the defence mechanism through which any subject is stripped of its emotional content by intellectualising it.

In the phallic phase, there is *conversion*, that is, the displacement of dangerous content on to the body, targeting an organ that has some symbolic significance with regard to the content itself.

When the dangerous content is displaced on an object external to the body, we speak of *displacement*, which stands as the origin of transference (the emergence of what is repressed through transference allows for its interpretation).

When some content is avoided, orientating it towards an external object of opposite polarity, we speak of *condensation* (for example, I avoid feeling angry about the wickedness of a person by thinking about his goodness).

In the last developmental phase, that of latency, the person can defend himself through *sublimation* (that is, by transferring his own libidinal or aggressive burden to objects considered socially acceptable) and through *regression*, which is the return to a previous phase of libidinal development in the face of a conflict that is not otherwise resolvable. Although regression is typical of the latency, or adolescent, phase, which facilitates a recycling of the previous phases to prepare for entry to genital maturity, this is a defence mechanism that can also be used in each of the previous phases.

From a psychic point of view, each person has his own armoury of defences that he tends to favour over others; in other words, we all have defences that do not, in themselves, have a pathological connotation. We start to speak of pathology when the person becomes more rigid in his defences, thus impeding the activation of the functioning of the adult.

In an early phase, defence is very useful: it is the way in which a person gives meaning to the world and it allows the person to face it; nevertheless, this becomes a problem when the person uses that same defence constantly, and in a rigid way, to enable him to face the world and give it meaning.

Therefore, each type of psychopathology is characterised by the presence of a typical group of defences (Novellino, 1991). For example, in *schizophrenia*, we find defences which are typical of the oral phase, with the addition of regression and the defences of the later periods when there is a neurotic cover for the schizophrenia; in depression, typically we find denial, projective identification (if the depression is psychotic), and introjection, which takes the characteristic of *turning against the self*.

Again, in *obsessive neurosis*, we find all the defences typical of the anal phase, while, in the *phobic* type, displacement and condensation prevail.

The so-called *cover defences*, or, rather, those defences which mask a more serious psychiatric pathology, can be explained by turning to the concept of "fixation" in a particular phase of development: each person has areas of fixation in a phase of development prior to that in which he finds himself; in this area, he uses the defences typical of the phase in which he has become fixated. These defences are functional because they prevent the person from slipping into a previous phase of development, in which a much more serious conflict might have developed. When these defences fail, the person slips into the previous phase of development and comes into contact with the hidden conflict. This can be correlated with the transactional analytic concept of *impasses*: an *impasse* of the first degree often masks a more serious impasse of the second and third degree, and, therefore, the first serves as a defence against the more deeply hidden conflict. It is, consequently, risky to work on impasses and on cover defences before resolving the underlying conflict.

Counter-resistance. Analysis of countertransference

The phenomenon of countertransference is of great clinical importance in understanding *counter-resistance*. The model that is most useful in dealing with this goes back to the concept of *internal dialogue*, through which Kahler (1978) describes two possible routes for its use.

The first is that of *introjection*, in which the person projects on the other person his own parent, energising the "Adapted Child" in such a way that the person who is the object of projection assumes socially the role of the Parent (in depressed patients, this allows the patient to liberate himself from his own "Persecutor Parent"); the second possibility, that defined as *projection*, is that the Parent interacts directly with the Child of the other person: it is assumed that such a manoeuvre works because the person "hooks" a Child equivalent to his own, creating in this way a sort of symbiosis.

Sequence of internal dialogue (Kahler)

Projective: the sender energises his own Parent, soliciting in the receiver the AC. Introjective: the sender energises his own AC (Victim) and projects on the receiver his own Parent, so that the receiver activates his own Parent (Rescuer or Persecutor), leaving his own AC internalised.

In psychological games, what occurs is that the players alternate between the projective and introjective mechanisms, typically changing modality at the moment their roles change.

In terms of transference and countertransference, this signifies that, in applying this type of model, we have the possibility of reading, in terms of sequence of projection and introjection, what is verified in relationships.

The important point to remember is that, for these manoeuvres to be successful, it is necessary that there is an identification: in other words, for a Persecutor (psychologically a Victim) to be successful in his own manoeuvre to find an external Victim, it is necessary that the other has, in turn, an equivalent internal dialogue (for example: the depressed person who meets a therapist who has an internal dialogue of the type "you are not worthy enough") and, therefore, there is a reciprocal "identification", that is to say, a mirroring of roles and contents.

We speak of *negative countertransference* when there are unresolved experiences of the therapist that are transferred to the patient. This situation is the basis of a break-up of the therapeutic alliance, since it gives way to a *counter-resistance* which transmogrifies into a stagnation of the relationship. The phenomena which give rise to this occurrence derive from the unresolved processes that determine an identification process that the therapist recognises, or thinks he recognises, in the other part of himself.

Identification can be "concordant" or "complementary" (Novellino, 1984a).

Concordant identification refers to the phenomenon through which the therapist recognises himself as a reflection of the patient, and feels that which the patient feels: if the patient is depressed, the therapist also feels depressed.

Complementary identification describes the phenomenon that occurs when the therapist recognises himself in the role that the patient attributes to him, for example, a Negative Normative Parent, and is the result of that manoeuvre which Kahler defines as "introjective".

Concordant identification: the therapist identifies with the Child of the patient (Child–Child).
Complementary identification: the therapist identifies with the Parent of the patient (Parent–Child).

Another type of identification, connected to *complementary identification*, but typical of the borderline personality, is *alternating identification*, in which the patient is alternately the Child who projects his Parent on the therapist and, in a successive phase, the Parent who projects his Child on the therapist.

The importance of the concept of identification is that the therapist, recognising that which occurs in himself, has the opportunity to hypothesise, at the level of a reflection, *that which occurs in the patient*. The stimulus of the patient has a tendency to evoke a certain type of ego state in the other—in the therapist—as each type of functional style of ego state evokes mainly a complementary one (NP$\Rightarrow$AC, etc.).

In this way, if the patient communicates to the therapist: "You are not worth anything because up to now you haven't done anything for me!", it can activate the Negative Adapted Child (AC) in the therapist, who will end up feeling sad, guilty, and with the desire to send the patient to another therapist. If, instead, the therapist becomes aware of his countertransference reactions, recognising them for what they are, he will leave his own Adult active and will ask himself what is happening and what the reason is for this reaction (otherwise, he risks remaining in the Adapted Child situation, therefore entering into symbiosis); thanks to his Adult, the therapist can recognise from his own reaction (*own AC-"solicited": social and phenomenological diagnosis of the ego states*) that the patient is projecting his Negative Normative Parent, and can be in tune with the Negative Adapted Child of the patient and establish a strategy that uses both ego states of the patient (NP and AC) which are active at that moment.

The feeling of "unworthiness" of the therapist is, in the final analysis, a signal that indicates a conflict between the Parent and the Child *of the patient* caused by the presence of an internal dialogue that is closed off and rejecting *in the patient*. The therapist might not readily perceive this, but that would imply that he is defending himself and that he should look for the reason in his own script. The therapist, too, is putting into action defences which probably go back to a developmental phase of around two to three years of age, and even if the therapist has successfully dealt with such a phase in general, he can, nevertheless, relive something which becomes activated by the patient if he is "in tune" with the latter.

> The therapist has three sources of data to help him understand the patient: listening, observation, and the reactions which the patient stirs up inside him.

What, however, are the possibilities of self-analysis on the part of the therapist?

When phenomena of countertransference arise, the therapist is obliged both to become aware of them, but not to collude with them, and to use the material which comes to him through the countertransference as an important source of data to help him work with the patient.

> The clinical evidence demonstrates that when the therapist enters into a relationship of countertransference that he does not succeed in developing, statistically, his probability of error rises, even in situations which otherwise he would have known how to develop competently. This is because, until the countertransference is developed, his actions are contaminated by the child.

Self-analysis can be carried out by the therapist through a comparison between the actual situation and the content of the script of which he is aware. The therapist can ask himself questions, such as:

> "I get angry with the patient because he does not change: in which situations of my past did something similar occur?"
> "Who did I not succeed in changing in my childhood?"
> "What caused me to suffer sadness or delusion when I was young?"

Through this modality, which is essentially a *historical analysis of ego states*, the therapist might discover, for example, that when he was young his father used to get angry with him when he made a mistake, and, therefore, his present anger comes from his Parent; or he could find that he himself, when he was young, got angry with his younger sister, and, therefore, his present anger comes from the Child. If the historical diagnosis does not reveal the cause of his anger, a *phenomenological diagnosis* from experience is necessary, and this is something that is inadvisable to do alone: supervision, or even a resumption of therapy, will be necessary, focused on that area.

Another question the therapist could ask himself might be, "Who does this patient remind me of?"

This question has the objective of separating the person and the patient from the ghosts that the therapist projects on to him.

In essence, the key question to ask yourself each time is:

> "In what way does this patient, or what he is doing, fall within in my script?"

Once the therapist uses as a model of interpretation that which is based on identification, and, therefore, hypothesises that that which occurs in him is a reflection equivalent to that which is occurring in the patient, then he will be able to plan an equivalent intervention (the technique of the two-chairs work, an interpretation or another).

The triadic approach to resistance

The concept of resistance comes from the theory and the practice of Freudian psychoanalysis, and is classically defined as "everything which holds back the patient from exposing material which comes from the unconscious" (Fenichel, cited in Novellino, 1998).

From a historical point of view, it is interesting to point out that two of the principal post-Freudian psychotherapies (that of Gestalt therapy and of transactional analysis) have adopted radically different attitudes with respect to this clinical phenomenon, as is evident in the works of the two founding fathers (respectively, Fritz Perls and Eric Berne). In Gestalt therapy, resistance is considered to be the principal point of the therapeutic work, whereas in classical transactional analysis, resistance was undervalued, or at any rate not taken explicitly into account, until the mid-1980s.

The first author who set about tackling the problem of resistance in transactional analysis was Drye (1974), a transactional analyst with a background in psychoanalysis. Drye highlighted the functional (behavioural) aspect of the phenomenon of resistance, identifying the Rebellious Child ego state as being responsible for its expression. Furthermore, he illustrated the effectiveness of therapeutic intervention aimed at the recovery of the alliance with the patient, carried out through recognition of the positive intention behind the rebellious behaviour.

A functional point of view also characterises the approach to resistance taken by Dusay (in Barnes, 1977); he emphasises that its manifestation reveals another function of the Adapted Child in the egogram of the patient.

If, so far, we have considered *resistance as an expression of the Child ego state*, a student of Schiff, Mellor (1980), has emphasised the importance of the Parent ego state in such a process: this can, in fact, have caused the incorporation of messages of the type "I must not listen to you", or "Don't tell me what I should do". If this is the case, the intervention chosen should be the *Parent Interview*.

With the objective of the psychotherapeutic intervention in mind, it can be useful to identify three levels of the phenomenon of resistance in psychotherapy. These are, the intrapsychic one of the patient, the intrapsychic one of the therapist, and the culture in which the patient–therapist couple operate.

The following classification (Novellino, 1998), relative to the levels just listed, has the aim of stimulating further reflection and study on the subject:

- Resistance in the patient
  - pre-therapeutic (learning deficit, impasses)
  - therapeutic ("therapeutic impasses")
  - post-therapeutic
- Resistance in the therapist
  - technical incompetence and/or cultural prejudice
  - collusion
  - incompatibility with the patient
- Systemic resistance
  - of the environment (cultural script)
  - of the family (family script).

Let us consider now in more detail the so-called forms of resistance.

The concept which should be underlined is that which defines resistance as a "triadic" phenomenon (Novellino, 1998): resistance to change in therapy is a function of the interaction between the resistance of the patient, of the therapist, and of the system.

In a case in which the patient is induced to undertake a psycho-therapeutic treatment, what he will show during the sessions is, therefore, the *fusion* of his own intrapsychic resistance with a resistance of the system (couple, family, culture in a wide sense).

The first task of the psychotherapist must then be to evaluate which of the two forms of resistance is predominant in determining and/or reinforcing the psychological problem of the patient, and, therefore, to orientate the intervention towards an action on the person (individual or group psychotherapy) and/or on a system (family or couple therapy).

At the level of the *intrapsychic resistance of the patient*, what occurs is that he will be affected either by a learning deficit or by an *impasse* (in reality, the two situations are always present contemporaneously, even if in different measures).

Resistance can, therefore, be considered as the functional aspect of the impasse, which is a concept of structural order.

If the impasse can be the cause of resistance before the therapy, it can also be so during the therapy itself (therapeutic impasse). A clinical example will help to better illustrate the concept.

A, a patient aged thirty-five, comes to psychotherapy complaining about difficulty in "controlling" her anger in interpersonal relationships, insomnia, depression, anxiety about the future, a lack of commitment in her work, and a series of intimate relationship failures.

She presents as alternately seductive and hostile; her games are mainly "Rapo" and "Now I've got you, you son of a bitch"; the script matrix contains messages from the counter-script such as "be perfect" and "please me", injunctions such as "don't be important" and "don't exist", and a programme that instructs her to "be independent from men".

During the first phase of work (the contractual objective is that of "recognising and managing the impulses of anger"), the impasses of the first degree (between "please me" and "I want to be important") are confronted and resolved by working on decontamination; the patient learns to recognise the external and internal stimuli which lead her to a racket of anger, and to understand the underlying pain. After an immediate improvement in both mood and insomnia, which helps to alleviate problems with interpersonal relationships, there follows a new period of depression and demotivation, with feelings of distrust of the therapy. Confronting these emotions through an analysis both of internal dialogue and of a dynamic of the transference, an impasse becomes evident between the cognitive re-decision that resulted from the previous work on the impasse of the first type ("I have the right to feel important") and the injunction "do not be important". In addition to the interpsychic resistance, there is a systemic resistance: her mother and her elder sister react to her greater assertiveness, making her feel guilty and insinuating doubts about the therapy. The therapeutic work with this patient concentrates, therefore, on the feeling of guilt and on her infant origins; what emerges, through a detailed analysis of the transference dynamic, is a protocol, going back to four or five years of age, during which the patient had experienced a demolition of the paternal figure by the mother, and, therefore, a feeling of guilt for loving the father. Then, aided by regressive work, the re-decision becomes, "I have a right to have feelings different from mum . . . I am different to her . . .".

The *post-therapeutic resistance* can be caused by three principal factors.

The first is the result of a lack of work on integration, which characterises the final phase of the psychotherapeutic process.

In practice, the new data and the new potential available to the person are not sufficiently aligned and integrated with the old system of reference, thus impeding co-operation and support among the different parties.

The second factor can be the opposition of a systemic resistance to the changes obtained in therapy: in this case, the cultural script countermands the stabilising re-decisional process.

The third factor consists of a process definable as "therapeutic regression from stress". In fact, the re-decisional process consists of leading the person as far as possible towards the OK pole on the "decisional scale" (Woollams & Brown, 1978), in a way that allows him to react in a functional manner to the stress normally present in *his* system. If this exceeds the acquired capacity to tolerate it, in which case a return to the systemic resistance will occur, there will be a regression manifested by the script.

Let us now analyse the phenomenon of *resistance in the psychotherapist*. Without having any intention of furnishing a complete and definitive list, here are some causes which seem to be among the most frequent.

That which is most widespread is professional incompetence, caused both by an incapacity to lead the patient through the work set out in the various strategic phases, and by failing to achieve a therapeutic resolution of important contamination.

If we follow Freudian teaching, we should always remember that:

> no therapist will lead the patient beyond where he himself has arrived.

The point about competence can be further broadened by the capacity (and ethics) of the psychotherapist to evaluate the potential and energy required with regard to that patient. The key question is:

> "Am I the right therapist for this patient?"

At this level, the "incompetence" also includes the non-evaluation of a possible incompatibility with the patient.

Finally, principally, the phenomenon of *collusion* appears to be central.

By this, we mean a situation in which an aspect of the personality of the patient, generically or specifically, reflects an unresolved problem of the therapist, who does not become aware of it. This last point is fundamental. Which therapist, in front of a depressed patient, say, does not experience, to a greater or lesser extent, his own depressive nucleus? Becoming aware, through the subsequent work of separation of the self and the other, allows the therapist to avoid harmful effects, such as projection that is not reappropriated on his part.

Without doubt, it is becoming aware of, and mastering, collusions that determine one's ability to become a psychotherapist, something that is far beyond the mere learning of technique.

Resistance in groups and anti-leadership

Two frequent situations of group resistance are described, in the form of opposition to the leader of the group (Novellino, 1985a).

In the first situation, a member of the group places himself in *open* opposition to the therapist. Clinical example:

Therapist (T): Describes during the first meeting of the group the rules of the structure of the group, among which is the commitment to pay the fees of all of the sessions.

Client (C): "This rule does not seem fair to me. It does not take into account that something can happen to anyone, it is too rigid."

T: "Express what you feel."

C: "This seems to me to be a manipulation! What do the others think?"

The therapist subseqently chooses to introduce, as a therapeutic manoeuvre, the game of "Courtroom". In the following work carried out with the client, together with the group that confronts him, his script decision emerges: "Here [in the family] I am not well . . . but if I try to rebel, I can resist that label!"

The example given is chosen to highlight some of the characteristics of the dynamic situation definable as *anti-leadership alpha*. This consists of an *open opposition to the leader* (therapist) and the social objective is to remove from him the effective leadership (or subleadership, according to Berne). The client usually makes transactions directed at the therapist with his "Rebellious Adapted Child", and even when he makes transactions with the other members of the group, the object of these, too, is something to do with the therapist. As a result of these transactions, they often play games ("Courtroom", "Now I've got you, you son of a bitch"), which normally remain at the first and second degree of resistance. In the therapy work carried out with clients of this type, the main themes that emerge go back to the Oedipal phase, and the most recurrent script decisions can be summarised in the formula: "I will show the world how imperfect you are", and the feelings involved go back to racket about *jealousy*. These clients present personality organisations of the neurotic type. With this type of client, it is important to recognise the positive intention of aggression, which usually consists of making positive affirmations of being a capable and mature person in the eyes of the parents; an intervention aimed at stroking the "Rebellious Child" (Drye, 1974) helps, therefore, to therapeutically confront the anti-leadership action.

In the second type of anti-leadership, a dynamic situation takes place that is highly pathological and destructive for the process of the group. It usually involves a client who has a marginal or paranoid personality organisation who conducts a very *veiled* competition with the therapist, with the aim of *taking on the psychological leadership of the group*. The process is rather long and is enacted through the psychological level of the transactions. The client does not show open transactions of verbal aggression to the therapist, and he limits himself to non-verbal carom transactions, in which the message circulated to the members of the group and to the therapist is "you are getting everything wrong (. . . I will show you how you bad are)" through slight signals of disapproval regarding the way the therapist is operating. A typical signal of this phenomenon during the group process is the isolation of the client during moments of group activity and of intimacy in the group. The problems that emerge during the work with this type of client go back to the *oral phase* (envy). During this type of dynamic, what often occurs is that, in other members of the group, fantasies and themes of a depressed type re-emerge ("I think that I will not succeed anyway . . . that the group is not useful", etc.).

If the essential position of the anti-leader alpha is I'm OK—You're not OK (I'm not OK—You're OK at the psychological level), in the anti-leader beta, the essential position that emerges is I'm not OK—You're not OK ("given that nothing is worth it, I will destroy myself by destroying you").

We are, therefore, faced with a very serious situation that can slip into games of the third degree (for example, attempts at suicide on the part of the client). Such dynamics need to be dealt with using multiple techniques, with continuous attention to the process that the client is carrying out, and, in particular, to the fact that: (1) he continues to accumulate anger; (2) he is becoming deprived of strokes; (3) he is heading towards a tragic end of the script; (4) he is facilitating the re-emergence of psychotic nuclei in other members of the group.

The work method should be aimed at rendering the aggression social and explicit (destructive anger), for example, contrasting with the isolation, and, in parallel, closing off the tragic exit, perhaps using a fantasy of the script ("what will happen if you continue not to work on yourself?") followed by re-decisional/interpretative work (Table 4).

Table 4. Types of anti-leadership aggression directed at two types of therapist.

α (alpha)	β (beta)
Social competition with T	Psychological competition with T
Transactions directed at the leader	Carom transactions towards the leader (including non-verbal)
Games of the first and second degree	Up to games of the third degree
Aggression of the Oedipal type (jealousy)	Aggression of the oral type (envy)
Leans towards sub-leader position	Psychological leader
Primary position: I'm OK/ You're not OK	Primary position: I'm not OK/ You're not OK

CHAPTER FOUR

The clinical methodology

Therapeutic plan and methodology

First of all, the difference between *therapeutic plan* and *methodology* has to be explained: the latter, in fact, refers to the clinical theory, which relates to the strategic phases in which the transactional theory can be applied to the psychotherapeutic setting, while the plan consists in the realisation of methodological principles in a particular clinical case (Novellino, 1998). Therefore:

- methodology is the theory underlying the techniques;
- therapeutic plan is the practice of the techniques.

Furthermore, psychotherapy, to keep itself within the boundaries of effectiveness, has to follow a *method* which takes into account the unique nature of the situation: the therapist, in fact, has to base his data, which he collects gradually, on this; it is precisely this collection of data and its deployment in coherent and demonstrable hypotheses which confers on psychotherapy its "scientific rigour" and "reproducibility".

Therapeutic contract and analytic contract: operative differences

The methodology's prime objective is to be realised in a therapeutic plan, which can be defined as that process which leads a contract of therapy to its conclusion.

The contracts of therapy are of two types (Novellino, 1998):

(a) contracts of social control: focal or reparation therapy
(b) contracts of autonomy: restructuring therapy/didactic analysis.

The social control contracts are those that have as their objective a behavioural change in the person (for example: for an agoraphobic to be able to leave the house, for a depressed person to be able to have friends and to keep a job), while the autonomy contract aims to recover autonomy in terms of awareness, spontaneity, and intimacy.

Therefore we can say that *social control* is the objective of a reparation or focal therapy with transactional analysis, while the *autonomy contract* calls more precisely for a restructuring therapy or an analytic therapy.

To speak of a therapeutic plan signifies, then, speaking of two different levels according to whether one refers to therapy or analysis, between which there is a substantial difference: we think, in particular, of the difference which exists between a contract of analysis for psychotherapists in training and a contract of therapy with neurotic or psychotic patients.

To characterise, we place these at two poles, at one extreme focal therapy, and at the other, didactic analytic therapy, with restructuring therapy being placed at an intermediate level:

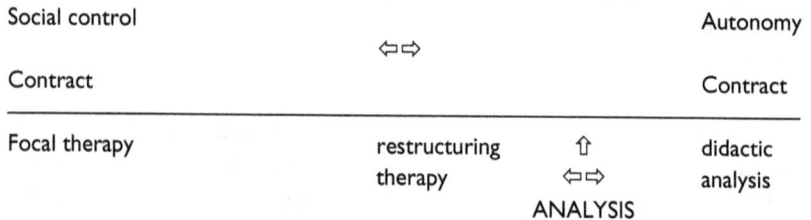

Social control			Autonomy
	⇦⇨		
Contract			Contract
Focal therapy	restructuring therapy	⇧ ⇦⇨ ANALYSIS	didactic analysis

Let us look at the points that characterise the important differences between a psychotherapy, primarily a focal one, and an analytic therapy.

Focal therapy		Analysis
	Contract	
Focal/social control		Autonomy
	Role	
Guide for focal objective		Guide to explore personality
	Transference	
Ignore/sustain positive transference		Elaborate positive and negative transference
	Unconscious	
Focus on conscious		Analysed

Remember that the *contract*, in the final analysis, is a means of defining the relationship. A contract of analysis will present aspects and implications different from those of a contract of therapy: in this way, for example, the analysis of dreams can be secondary in a contract of focal therapy.

Even *the role of the therapist* is very different: in focal therapy, the therapist helps the patient to define the problem, while, in analysis, there is the explicit agreement that not only what the patient describes as the problem will be explored, but also areas of which he is not aware and towards which he is ego-syntonic.

Another aspect that distinguishes these two processes is the different attitude regarding the *phenomena of transference*. In focal therapy, there are two options: that of not analysing the transference, or, alternatively, that of using it, even reinforcing the positive pole of the transference. In analysis (restructuring therapy or analytic psychotherapy), however, the transference is analysed, with regard to both the positive and the negative poles, and the therapist presents himself as an object of a projection and helps the patient to analyse it.

The final area of difference is the position regarding the *unconscious*. Here, it is necessary to make an explanatory statement: until now, the only form of psychotherapy which has developed a coherent model of techniques to obtain access to unconscious phenomena is psychoanalysis; everything that is done in the other therapies to gain access to the world of the unconscious is, in some way, borrowed from psychoanalysis. In order to gain access to the unconscious, psychoanalysis essentially has three instruments: dreams, free association, and the analysis of the phenomena of transference.

In transactional analysis the ways of accessing the unconscious are provided by:
(1)   analysis of dreams;
(2)   analysis of phenomena of transference and countertransference;
(3)   analysis of unconscious communication;
(4)   analysis by bioenergetic techniques of the body scripts.

The phenomena of transference and countertransference provide the therapist with a large mass of data about the unconscious of the patient and are understood in the broadest sense of the terms.

The body scripts, accessed through the reading of body language, say many more things about that which has been integrated at the unconscious level: a person who says he is satisfied with life, but walks bent-shouldered and dejectedly, reveals much about the burden of unhappiness he carries. The work dedicated to body scripts is based on an integration between transactional analysis and techniques of a Reichian, or bioenergetic, derivation.

The difference between strategy and tactics

For a therapeutic or analytic plan to achieve its objectives requires, from beginning to conclusion, a succession of strategic phases (the strategy is the direction taken to reach an objective and the tactics constitute the operative modality). For example: if the strategy is dictated by the need to reinforce the Adult of a patient, the tactic called for is three-chair work.

In a therapeutic plan, it is important to establish the strategy from the very beginning, and to leave the tactics until later.

Strategic phases of the therapist

In a methodology which calls for the use of transactional analysis, the four strategic phases are better recognised now (already described in Chapter Two):

- alliance
- decontamination
- deconfusion
- re-learning.

These phases should not be thought of as being linear, but as a *spiral*, because the work leads to the successive deepening of awareness of the problem. For example: at the beginning the problem can be constituted by an impasse of the first degree; consequently, an alliance is formed, a decontamination, a possible deconfusion, and the relative re-learning follow; successively, one will be faced with an impasse of the second degree, which requires a new alliance, and so on. This cyclical process, which the patient and the therapist experience as going backwards, is a sign that the therapy is proceeding, because the contents are becoming deeper. In this way, an anxiety which signals the presence of an impasse of the first degree might reappear after having been confronted and resolved in an earlier phase, but will indicate an impasse of the second degree, which will, in its turn, be confronted and resolved.

An obsessive patient, for example, will present his neurotic rituals at the beginning of the therapy, and then, having resolved these, will pass on to a phase in which the problem will be constituted by his relationships with others; then the problem will be caused by his feelings, and so on, in a way that always lies deeper, until he arrives at the central problem in the obsessive structure, which is caused by the necessity to maintain control.

Alliance

Psychotherapy is based on an "intense" relationship. At the beginning, when two persons meet, each one evaluates the other with his own A1 (Little Professor) to decide whether that person is an adequate partner, and, at that point, the relationship is established. It does not remain passively stable, however, but, for both partners, there follows work of reciprocal recognition and realignment and successive inter-relationships, based on which the relationship either remains stable or deteriorates. This also happens in therapy: after the initial alliance is stablised during the therapy, there is a progressive deepening of the theme, and this determines the necessity of re-examining the alliance, giving the patient the opportunity either to invest his trust in the therapist again or not to do so.

This can also be explained in terms of transference: remember that *transference* is the projection of the patient's Parent to the therapist. Now, every Parent is a structure composed in reality of the image of the parental figures in different developmental periods and derived from different relationships with the paternal figures; in this way, we have a Parent that corresponds to the oral phase, one that corresponds to the anal phase, and so on. As the dynamics become more profound, the patient projects to the therapist parental images constructed in different developmental phases, and, therefore, he will have different expectations, corresponding to the phase in which he finds himself, and the therapist has to respond to the patient's demands in an adequate way, otherwise he will not maintain the alliance. Then the patient projects the other "bad" polarity of the Parent, causing anxiety in both himself and the therapist, a break-up of the preceding alliance, and the possible constitution of a new one.

> Constructing the alliance should be seen at two levels, social and psychological, and the competence of the therapist is tied to the success of making the two levels coherent. The social level has as an objective the construction of a contract with an adult–adult exchange.
>
> The psychological level is that of the transference alliance, which is played out in Parent–Child terms.

This level is not explicit, but the therapist should be aware of it, because the patient's Child accepts the therapist's Parent as a valid substitute for the actual parent.

Berne, in an article that appeared in *Bulletin* in 1962, describes the phases of this introjective process. He asserts that, in the first phase, the Little Professor of the patient's Child studies the therapist's Parent to perceive whether or not he is a valid substitute for the actual Parent: for this reason, in the early sessions, it is important that the therapist does not confront the patient or make premature interventions.

In the second phase, the patient accepts the therapist as a valid parental substitute and experiences the therapist's Adult as that Parent, whom he always felt he needed.

In the third phase, the patient realises that that which he had exchanged for Parent in the therapist is, in reality, an Adult, and, at this point, he can better understand the nature of the real transactions between himself and the therapist.

In the fourth phase, the patient realises that he also has an Adult capable of functioning as the therapist's Adult functions.

In the fifth phase, finally, the patient begins to make his Adult function and he will make use of it to detach himself from the therapist.

To effect a transference alliance, the tactic essentially consists of recognising and answering the psychological message, and, thus, not leaving the Child unheard. The demands of the patient have a social component of the Adult–Adult type, and a psychological one of the Child–Parent type (see Figure 1); the answer to the only social transaction, in fact, crosses that transaction.

For example:

Patient: "Doctor, how long will it take?" (Adult–Adult) (social level).
Patient: (Reassure me!) (Child–Parent) (psychological level).

If the therapist answers, "It is not possible to establish with certainty" (Adult) (social and psychological level), he crosses the transaction at the psychological level and the alliance cannot take place; if, instead, the therapist answers, "It will depend on the work we do together" (Adult at the social level, while the Parent at the psychological level sends a message saying something like: "I am listening to you and I will take care of you"), in this way, it allows the transaction to remain complementary, respecting the first rule of communication (Berne, 1961), and so allows the alliance to construct itself.

The alliance is, without doubt, influenced by the tactics of the therapist, but the global feeling of trust in the therapist as a parental substitute depends essentially on the empathy of the therapist (whose

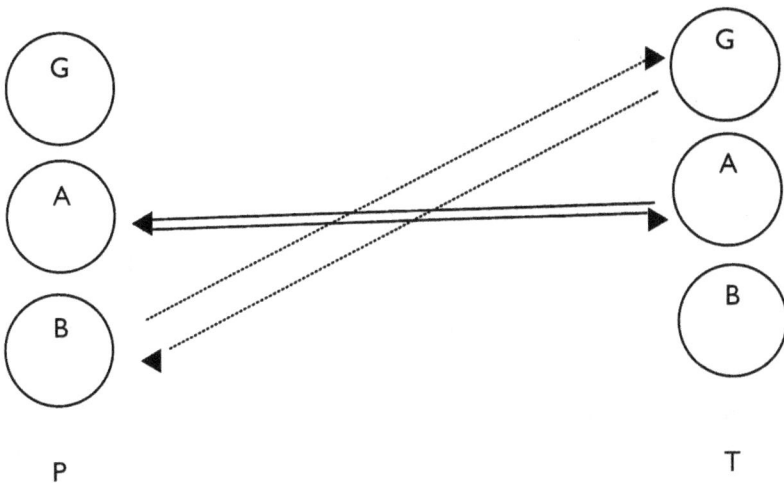

Figure 1.   Realising a transference alliance.

extra-verbal flow is of the Child–Child type), on his capacity to answer with all three of his ego states.

Decontamination

This phase and that of deconfusion are the two central phases of the therapy and can be understood theoretically by applying the concept of *impasse*.

Impasse, in structural terms, can be defined as an unresolved conflict between Parent and Child; this conflict contaminates the Adult, preventing it from functioning with awareness and effectiveness. Until the impasse is resolved, this produces a double contamination, in which the Parental pole is signified by a script message and the Child pole by an unsatisfied need. This implies that until the person experiences the material of the impasse as imposed by a real situation, he will experience the problem as ego-syntonic ("I am made like that"). He needs, therefore, a first phase of decontamination in which the strategic objective is that of constructing a situation in which the patient becomes aware that the material that he thought was Adult actually pertains to the Parent and to the Child. Strategically, the decontamination serves to create an "observing" ego, which, in the next phase, is capable of observing the old material in the here-and-now and, thus, is able to resolve it. Focal psychotherapy stops at this stage.

Deconfusion

This is the strategic phase which leads to the resolution of the *impasse*; the conflict is resolved and integrated. The aim of the pschotherapy is to "deconfuse" the Child of the patient.

Deconfusion is achieved tactically:

- through the cutting and the *disconnecting of rubber bands* (Erskine, 1974), through the classical *re-decision technique* of the Gouldings (1979), and other classical techniques, such as dream-work and re-decision through body work;
- through the *Bernean operations* carried out until interpretation and crystallisation occur: it should be noted that the organisation of the pre-Oedipal personality is regressive and tends to split if subject to regressive techniques.

Relearning

Once the person reaches the re-decision, there is the final phase of relearning, which constitutes the concrete putting into action and the reinforcement of the changes established during the re-decision process. The strategic aim of relearning is that of creating a bridge between re-decision and social reality, between therapy and reality, and, therefore, to implement outside the group or the room of the therapist that which was re-decided.

The tactics are decided through the exercises of the group, through homework, and through what are known as the "social control contracts".

The relearning phase is of great clinical importance, because what happens after the re-decision is that the person has an old Parent with old orders and prohibitions, and a new Parent, who gives new permissions, but that the patient has to reinforce to be able to trust.

A game should be mentioned here, frequently used in the relearning phase: "It's too soon to terminate" (O'Leary, 1969). This consists in delaying the end of the therapy because of a re-emergence of old symptoms or the emergence of new problems. The analysis of this game consists of making explicit the anxiety of abandonment present in the patient–therapist relationship, in order to constructively facilitate the separation.

Casalegno (2005) has illustrated, in a valuable work, the *conclusion of the therapy as a strategic under-phase in relearning*. The author highlights the following objectives:

- elaboration of the experiences of the separation;
- elaboration of possible negative unresolved transference;
- consolidation of trust in oneself;
- acceptance of the limits of the therapy;
- separation from the therapist.

CHAPTER FIVE

The setting

*Premise: the six steps of the first interview and
the setting in transactional psychoanalysis*

The aim of this premise (Novellino, 2010) is to put straight the principles of transactional analysis, orientated in a psychodynamic sense and applied to how the phase of the initial interview is carried out. The concepts described by Berne are taken up again, integrated both with some of the literature of transactional analysis, and with Langs' methods of communicative psychoanalysis. The construction of the setting as a moment founded on an alliance of effective work is highlighted from both a methodological and a tactical point of view.

I present, first of all, the questions to which I requre an answer through a psychodynamic approach:

- In what way can transactional analysis proceed from decontamination to deconfusion?
- Which specific steps should be taken by transactional analysts in applying the Bernean principles (1966) to an individual setting?

- In the therapeutic relationship, *what does working on the psychological script imply,* referring to it in the way that Berne conceptualised it, or as a derived transference from infantile vicissitudes (1961)?
- Which borders should be established between psychotherapy and counselling?

This fourth point is particularly topical today. The borders between psychotherapy and counselling are hotly debated: the definitions of counselling vary, a little like a blanket that is too short, confusing itself sometimes with brief and supporting psychotherapy. The result is that we see psychotherapists who do counselling, and counsellors who do psychotherapy; just as we see schools of psychotherapy that, in reality, turn out counsellors, and schools of counselling that turn out psychotherapists.

In as much as there is a universal agreement on contractuality as the foundation of the therapeutic relationship between transactional analyst and patient, it is, nevertheless, surprising to me how little work there is that highlights the level of importance that Berne gave to the contract phase (1961, 1966): certainly he viewed it as an agreement on the therapeutic objectives in a strict sense, but also, and above all, as the construction of a work "environment" in which the therapist and the patient collaborate in analysing the unveiling of the script. If, on the one hand, the works dedicated to the first aspect, the therapeutic objective, can be counted in hundreds, on the other hand, the works referring to the second aspect, the construction of the "environment", can be counted on the fingers of two hands.

In my opinion, the risk with this is that we might move away from the rigour that Berne applied to the initial co-ordinates of a therapeutic relationship.

This section intends, therefore,

- to cover the set-up of the contract, as proposed by Berne;
- to reconsider those authors who followed the global message and went beyond the purely technical aspect;
- to propose finally a clear and applicable methodology with which to construct a work setting that develops, in a psychodynamic sense, the phase of the initial interview, particularly if the result indicates that an individual psychotherapy is needed.

Berne applied an innovative approach to his psychoanalytic roots, and, together with other areas of his theory, to the therapeutic alliance.

As I have already highlighted above, he gave to the concept of the contract a broader significance than that universally recognised but only partially implemented, in order to establish therapeutic objectives that were shared and verifiable.

As early as 1962, in an article perhaps seldom referred to, he asks himself and us an essential question:

> "When is it that the patient is really in therapy?"

His answer is that it is surely when the patient has made a *commitment*, but the interesting thing he goes on to say is that he does not only refer to a commitment made with the Adult ego state, but also through a process which involves the Child ego state of the patient. The patient is in therapy when his Child has accepted the Adult of the therapist as a valid substitute for his own Parent; in other words, he perceives the therapist as a more protective parent than that which he has introjected from his actual parental figures. In this first phase of the therapeutic relationship, described by Berne as delicate and unstable, but necessary, we can witness a "transference improvement"; a "real improvement" can take place only in the subsequent relational phase, in which the patient realises that what he had perceived as a Parent is, in reality, the Adult of the therapist. In the third phase, the patient will learn to count on his own Adult, being able in this way to detach himself from the therapist. In essence, Berne describes a relational process that is developed on psychodynamic bases. He describes a process which consists of *three successive psychological divorces*: the Child of the patient "divorces" first his own old Parent, then the Parent of the therapist, and, finally, also the Adult of the latter. Therefore, the Child transfers his need for support from his own old Parent to his own Adult, experiencing the Adult of the therapist as a valid intermediary.

In 1966, Berne systemises, in his book on the principles of group therapy, the methodology of transactional analysis. In the second chapter, dedicated to the "preparation of the scene", he conceives the contract as a process with three levels, interdependent between themselves. The first is *administrative*, where the "rules of the game" are defined; the second is *professional*, which lays out the objectives of the therapy itself; the third is *psychological*, tied to the needs and to the implicit expectations.

I present once more the assertions of Berne (1966), which laid down the objectives of the first interview:

- in the contract between therapist and patient both the commitment of the therapist ("My work here is to . . .") and the commitment of the patient ("My reason in coming to this group is . . .") should be clarified (p. 19)
- the therapist should assure himself that the interested parties are clarified both on the limits and the potential which the treatment can offer (professional contract), and on the practical requests of the therapeutic situation (administrative contract) (p. 20)
- the therapist should maintain an attitude of autocorrection (p. 22). He must be a navigator: "It is only the amateur who thinks that his compass always points to the North; the professional presumes that there will be deviations and he wants to know the corrections which he has to make each time he reads it" (p. 23)
- the therapist should limit the external information about his own patient (p. 36), to maintain the liberty to make his own image of the latter relying on his own intuition and experience.

With regard to the first of Berne's metaphors, that of the therapist as a navigator, I note an analogy with clinical material which is emerging from the theory of "sloppiness" applied to transactional analysis (Novellino, 2008). In this theory, the necessity for the therapist to understand the element of inevitable unpredictability that is inherent to the development of the therapeutic process is emphasised.

The first author to reconsider the importance of the setting after the death of Berne was James (1977).

She writes,

Even the therapist's clothes and office setting affect the process of decontamination. Experienced therapists are aware that anything they say or do, including how they decorate their offices, is a stimulus to one or more of their client's ego states. (p. 96)

She, therefore, dwells on different aspects of the environment of the therapy room; colours, paintings, arrangement of the armchairs, even providing alternative suggestions useful for creating a protective and welcoming environment. Regarding the first interview, James is one of the few authors to provide specific information. First of all, she clarifies that, as a standard approach is not definable, the preferred method in transactional analysis is that of proposing an "open" interview, in which the patient is left free to express spontaneously his own reasons, intervening thereafter with specific questions to focus on the areas which were neglected. She places the initial interview in a first phase with the aim of establishing a *work relationship* (p. 101). Some of her practical suggestions are repeated here, since they are germane to the present work:

- [it is] important to clarify the source of the referral;
- the fees and the modalities of payment are to be quickly defined;
- transactional analysis is to be synthetically explained as to how it will be used;
- it is useful to keep a blackboard in the visiting room.

Another concept that James expresses, which is seldom present in the transactional analysis literature in general, is that of the *referral* to another therapist (p. 110). The referral is to be proposed:

- giving valid reasons to motivate acceptance of the referral;
- at an early moment, so as to limit the frustration and the sense of abandonment of the patient.

We have to jump to 1980 to find another work (by Cornell) that deals with the first interview. He specifies three main objectives:

- to establish the *commitment* and collaboration of the patient. To this end, he suggests using a conversational style, and, above all, that the therapist should open with the question: "What do you need to know about me?" (p. 5); this serves to give the patient the idea that he can choose and need not feel obliged to take up the therapy with the therapist who interviews him;
- to establish a *therapeutic rule*: this is achieved through what the therapist makes happen rather than from what he says; in other words, from the style that he gives to the therapeutic work;
- to identify the competence and the fragility of the patient.

Other authors who have given space to the set up of the environment are Clarkson (1992) and Hargaden and Sills (2003), all interested in a deepening of the psychodynamic level of the therapeutic relationship.

Clarkson (1992) talks about both a "microscopic" and a "macroscopic" perspective in the methodological applications of transactional analysis. Therefore, the author emphasises the importance of the non-verbal level (eyes, face, skin, breath, clothes), and also the *slip of the tongue*, on the subject of which she describes a beautiful clinical case, that of Peter (p. 91).

Another concept of Clarkson, which I find fits well with a way of understanding the setting in a psychodynamic sense, is the following. In the first minutes of the first interview, the structure is established, albeit in embryonic form:

- the therapeutic themes of the patient which will be developed in the course of months and years;
- the first impressions of the therapist who will organise his therapeutic plan.

In a macroscopic perspective, Clarkson talks about establishing a *work relationship*, and, in that sense, understands psychotherapy as an internal voyage, for which the psychotherapist does not have a map, but should have the capacity to draw maps. This capacity is based on his competence in respecting, and making the other respect, the reciprocal setting, and his capacity to manage variations in the setting itself.

Hargaden and Sills (2003) dwell on the *work alliance*. For these two authors, a work alliance is based on:

- a clear and shared agreement on the objective of the work;
- a clear understanding of how the therapy will function;
- an empathic union.

The first point refers to the therapeutic contract, the second to the setting.

Hargaden and Sills also take the therapy to mean a *voyage of discovery*, which, therefore, could extend beyond the limits of the initial therapeutic contract.

The tourist and the traveller. One can note how the different authors already referred to (Berne, Clarkson, Hargaden and Sills) use the metaphor of psychotherapy as a voyage. Well, then, I think we can extend this metaphor, illustrating:

- a *transactional analysis with a cognitive–behaviouralist orientation*, as represented in the activity of the *tourist*, or a structuring of the pre-organised time, which is tied to specific and predetermined therapeutic objectives;
- a *transactional analysis with a psychodynamic orientation*, comparable with the activity of self-exploration of the traveller, and, therefore, based on the centrality of the setting.

Both the tourist and the traveller want to undertake a route marked by a departure and an arrival, but conceive in different ways the manner in which they will realise and experience the route.

Transactional pyschoanalysis. Moiso and I (1982) have introduced in the transactional-analytic literature the main methodological lines of the so-called "psychodynamic approach", characterised by the return to the analytic roots of Bernean work. This approach, applied to the reality of individual psychotherapy, takes the name of "transactional psychoanalysis" (Novellino, 2004), which is intended to highlight the methodological peculiarities to be considered in transferring the Bernean principles of group therapy (1966) to an individual setting.

As I have noted in previous writings (2003, 2004, 2005), this passage from a group setting to an individual one merits more explicit consideration than has hitherto been provided in the literature: this cannot consist of a mere automatic translation of the group setting. The present reflections on the psychodynamic conduct of the first interview are intended to provide further enlightenment on this subject.

A conceptual premise should first of all be constructed. In setting up a psychodynamic approach in transactional analysis, in particular when referring to individual psychotherapy, one should take into account the various contributions of the current movements in relational psychoanalysis (Novellino, 2004); however, in my opinion, that which ties in best with transactional analysis is that of communicative psychoanalysis (Langs, 1988).

From that viewpoint, I shall highlight the ideas which I consider to be central:

- the narratives of the patient should be seen as expressions in a symbolic code, called derivatives, of how the patient reads and experiences the therapist at an unconscious level, comparing what he says to what he does;
- the interpretation of these unconscious communications allows one to follow in an effective way how the patient relates his unconscious experiences in the therapeutic relationship;
- the expression of the derivatives and their correct interpretation are dependent primarily on the creation of an appropriate work setting;
- much research has demonstrated that it is the unconscious of the patient which indicates, and validates the principles of, appropriate settings that allow him to experience the therapist as a trustworthy and protective figure;
- these ideal rules, communicated by the unconscious of the patient, lead to the so-called psychotherapy of the secure frame, while any modifications to the ideal rules lead to the psychotherapy of the deviant frame;
- the capacity of the therapist to offer a "secure frame" that instils in the patient a sense of trust, because, through this, the therapist corresponds to the patient's unconscious expectations of the role that he should have: clear interpersonal limits, with good equilibrium between intimacy and distance; a healthy therapeutic symbiosis based on an introjection by the patient of the therapist as having a clear identity;
- the psychotherapy of the secure frame is that which best permits working through an interpretative approach that welcomes the unconscious expressions of the patient about the therapist, and, therefore, leads to a real gaining of consciousness.

If we are intending to integrate the fundamentals of the approach described above with transactional analysis, I think that it is important to point out that the latter orientation should be understood as a methodological proposal which defines a choice of field. I agree with Tudor (2002), who considers that presently in transactional analysis, two main methodological trends should be highlighted: (a) the *cognitive–behavioural* one, which makes reference to Berne in connection with decontamination; (b) the *psychodynamic* one, which draws on Berne with regard to deconfusion.

The two trends should co-operate, rather than compete, in the search for the most appropriate methodological assets (Steiner & Novellino, 2005):

- for a therapist, these would relate to his particular convictions, ideals, and values, and his personality structure;
- for a patient, the focus should be on his needs, on his script.

What should be avoided, in my personal opinion, are certain over-laps that are simplistic and might be damaging to the progress of the therapy. One example concerns the way of behaving when faced with *transference and countertransference phenomena*. I consider that in order to integrate the analysis of these phenomena, one needs a global revision of the way to set up the beginning of the therapeutic relationship and, therefore, of the *setting*: working with phenomena so profound and complex should not, and cannot, be dealt with by the simplified approach of tactics of "the moment". In other words, the analysis of transference is a question of method and not of technique.

Although for both of the methodological trends a contractual setting with rules is indispensable, there are fundamental differences, which I will summarise in the following way.

- In the cognitive–behavioural approach, the setting serves:
  (a) to avoid psychological games;
  (b) to keep the Adult energised with the aim of decontamination.
- In the psychodynamic approach, the setting:
  (a) constitutes the secure frame that allows for the expression of *transference and countertransference phenomena*;
  (b) provides a secure base for the emergence of unconscious dynamics and of their *interpretations*.

After a phase of marked resistance to the rediscovery of Berne's analytic roots, there was perhaps a movement towards a widespread and sometimes uncritical acceptance. Working on the *unconscious* of the patient calls for two essentials:

- the competence of the therapist in working on the unconscious;
- the awareness of the necessity of a protective holding, therefore a well-equipped setting.

Returning to the theme of the first interview set up in a psycho-dynamic perspective, let us now go through the specific points that will prove useful in recognising the characteristics of this approach. We shall consider, therefore, six successive phases (*the six steps of the first interview*) in which a budding relationship between a therapist and a potential patient can be established (Novellino, 2010).

The first phone call. The therapist should take into account that, at this point, the patient has already constructed a preconceived image based on how much he knew about the therapist during the referral phase, and this image will continue to form itself in the unconscious mind during the first phone call. The therapist should focus on two essential objectives:

- to check the *source of the referral*, in order to exclude possible situations that would immediately preclude taking that patient into therapy;
- to fix the first appointment.

The initial welcoming. Having met the potential patient in his practice, the therapist should take into account two factors that are interrelated: the physical environment and his own style of welcoming. Let us consider them separately.

The room of the therapist. Semi (1988), one of the researchers who has covered this aspect well, defines the room as:

> the physical container of the analytic situation . . . the dimensions, the organization of the space, the furniture and the atmosphere which it transmits reflect the characteristics of the contents which are peculiar to the analyst who lives there . . . the room, together with our look, our posture, our clothes, communicate to the patient our image. (p. 554)

Ideally, the room should be quiet and peaceful, be free from external intrusions, and be well separated from the house, or from the rooms of other professionals who could be sharing the premises.

The style of welcoming. To be able to offer a good therapeutic welcome, both during the first telephone call and at the first meeting, one needs to be aware of the suffering of the patient that has caused him to seek therapy. A patient might be seeking therapy for the first time, and, in this case, he usually does this after having first tried for months, or maybe for years, to "do it by himself"; another patient might have made a "pilgrimage" between many specialists (or non-specialists), and might feel deluded and disappointed by promises of miraculous cures. The therapist will take into account the state of anxiety and the need of the patient through his own sensitivity and empathy, and should appreciate that proposing a work method that calls for reciprocal commitment and constancy will partly reassure the patient and partly worry him. However, this is the only way to begin a working relationship which, in order to be constructive, has to replace in a convincing way both the illusions of a "novice" patient and the disappointments experienced by patients who have had previous therapy failures. Semi (1988) describes what Berne (1966) calls the *psychological contract* (1986) as an implicit exchange, and the premise of a good alliance:

> Patient: "I want to try to be that which I would like to be but which I am not."
> Therapist: "Accept being what you are, becoming that which you want to be as far as you can."

The therapist's explanation of making a therapeutic commitment. On the subject of this third step, let us recall how Berne (1966) explicitly considered it an essential factor in the construction of a therapeutic alliance. This third step in transactional analysis includes the therapeutic contract.

Enunciation of the basic rules. These must be explained, giving the patient the opportunity to present both his own conscious reactions and decisions (with the Adult) and the *derivatives of unconscious communication* mentioned earlier; in terms of time, this should take up not more than half of the first interview, if there are two, or of the second, if there are three. These have the objective of protecting both the patient and the therapist, and comprise:

1. The therapeutic space and the right interpersonal limits.
2. The modality of the relationship and, therefore, the treatment.
3. The capacity to offer a *holding*, and, therefore, an atmosphere of security.

The *rules of the secure frame* are characterised by:

1. *Firm and fixed rules* (Langs' *"fixed frame"*). These are unbreakable rules because they deal with the psychodynamic setting of the "secure frame", and once explained and accepted, have to remain the same. The rules define the provision of a stable and protective physical environment, the fee, and the frequency of the sessions (from one to (preferably) two a week), clarifying to the patient his responsibility to pay for the sessions (after having explained to him that the times are reserved exclusively for him);

2. *Flexible but stable rules*: these refer to the technical modality of the treatment, but, once established, are maintained: they include the possible use of the couch; the technique of free association; the free-flowing attention of the therapist and his "neutrality", meaning that he will abstain from making judgements and communications of a personal type. A possible *discretion* about the rule related to the responsibility of the patient to pay for the sessions should be evaluated case by case, but without discounting the dynamic implications which might ensue (Semi, 1988).

The therapist presents his own style of work. This serves to give the patient an idea from experience of how the work will proceed and the therapist the opportunity to verify from the beginning the adaptive reactions of the patient. There should be examples (Semi, 1988), of interpretative "sampling" interventions; also, the relating of a *first dream*, provided that it is very recent, is to be approved, particularly because this often contains embryonic themes of dynamic importance. For we transactional analysts, it is part of both self-presentation and the setting to provide a concise explanation of the theoretical model which will be used to facilitate a common language for what is to happen in the subsequent work.

Conclusion of the first interview. The patient is to be invited to a subsequent interview, in which he communicates his reaction and his *decision about the commitment*. It is generally agreed that it is preferable to ask for the *fee* at the end of the first interview, so that both parties can feel free with respect to the decision that the patient has to make.

Definition of setting

The *setting* is the whole of the rules that define the nature of the therapist–patient relationship, and is a fundamental premise of each form of psychotherapy.

In practice it is:

> all of the communicative behaviours with which the therapist defines the modalities according to which the therapy will take place: length and number of sessions, fee, skipped sessions, vacations, etc.

Remember that for patients regressed to the pre-Oedipal phase (marginal organisations and psychotic structures) who have particularly intense projective phenomena, there is a certain equivalence between setting and therapist:

Setting = Therapist

In other words, for the patient, the setting is seen as symbolising the therapist himself; in this way, for example, skipping a session is equivalent to an act of aggression against the therapist; a non-aggressive but symbiotic *agitation* can consist of an anxiety attack related to abandonment at the end of a session, expressed in an attempt to exceed the time limits. This can also be found in neurotic patients, although less intensely. *Any violation of the setting expresses peturbation towards the therapist and, as such, is to be analysed.*

Explanation of the setting. The rules of the setting are to be clearly defined at the beginning and the therapist will verify that they are understood and accepted by the patient.

The set-up of the case and the reference

Correctly setting up a clinical case is at the basis of therapy: exactitude here enhances the possibility of avoiding games and the probability of constructing a healthy alliance with the patient.

One aspect to consider is the *reference*: the *source of the referral* can provide excellent information about the motivation of the patient to "do therapy" and on any possible magical expectations of that patient.

Let us consider, for example, the patient who initiates contact with us with a sentence of this type: "I learned from Dr X that you are very competent, and I have come to you because I am *sure* that you can help me".

This sentence contains affirmations that indicate great (magical) expectations of the therapist, and that express the idea that the therapist will be able to resolve the case, thanks to his competence, with a consequent removal of any responsibility on the part of the patient: "*I* am *sure* . . . that *you* can help me."

Faced with such a situation, one has to seriously consider the possibility that the patient is playing a game of "Goodness, you're wonderful, Professor", which ends up with the therapist and the patient switching roles, with the patient in the role of Persecutor and the therapist in that of Victim as the game changes to one of "Corner".

Another example would be a patient sent by another patient already in therapy, or even a patient who was sent by someone who interrupted the therapy (dropped out). Patients who have issues to resolve with the therapist are particularly likely to send him other patients, with whom it is probable that the therapist finds himself having to "triangulate" at an unconscious level.

In the first type of referral, it is important to consider, for the patient already in therapy, whether the referral is a move in a game. The basic criterion is that of always first taking care of the patient whom the therapist still has and of analysing the dynamics with him: in general, during the analysis, something significant emerges and one discovers that the referral is a symbolic gesture with which the Child of the patient tries to communicate to the therapist something that he has difficulty putting into words: for example, it could be the need to "repair" an aggressiveness which he cannot express and about which he feels guilty.

In the case of the patient who has interrupted the therapy, there are two possibilities:

1. The patient has interrupted the therapy because he is convinced that he is well, and in this case the patient who is referred can have magical fantasies of the "wonderful professor" type regarding the therapist.
2. The patient has interrupted the therapy but continues to be unwell and, in this case, it is important to beware, because it is probable that the patient who is referred represents one of the moves of an aggressive game against the therapist.

One aspect, therefore, to which the therapist must pay attention when accepting the patient who is sent by a patient who has interrupted the therapy (particularly if this occurred because of a failure of the therapist) is *countertransference*: it can happen that the therapist has a reparation fantasy about his failure with the patient who dropped out of therapy. If this proves to be the case, the therapist should analyse the situation and take it into account (an example of *preformed counter-transference*).

Another possibility that one should always consider is that a patient might come not because of any real necessity, but because he has been influenced by societal customs (articles in newspapers, cultural habits, etc.); in such a case, before accepting the patient for therapy, it would be advisable to verify the clinical situation, the motivation, and the likelihood of change.

It is often the case that a patient comes to therapy because *someone else* has the objective of making him change (for example, the wife of the alcoholic who pushes her husband into therapy to make him stop drinking); in these cases there is a disparity between expectations and objectives which the therapist must clarify in a realistic way before accepting the patient into therapy.

Another classic situation is where a professional colleague refers a patient. In this type of referral, one should explore:

1. What the patient has experienced with the previous therapist(s).
2. What expectations have been created in him by the referring doctor.
3. Whether he knows about the relation between the referring doctor and the therapist, and if so, how he experiences it.

With regard to the first point, it should be taken into account that, if the patient has had a poor relationship with doctors, psychologists, or institutions that he feels have "treated him badly", he will come with *preformed* baggage of distrust with regard to his parents, which he will transfer directly to the therapist, accompanied by both feelings of hostility and expectations of repairing the "wrongs" suffered.

It is advisable to be wary of this *preformed transference*.

In conclusion, it is good practice always to ask the patient if he has had previous experiences with other therapists and, if the answer is affirmative, to ask how and why the relationship was interrupted.

The initial request

The initial request is extremely significant because it provides information about the script and about the motivation that the person has in coming to therapy.

Some patients do not make any request, but simply state the problem; there are also some who do not even state the problem and do not know how to describe the motivations for coming to us. Consequently, one must work to help the patient at this level.

The request can be made with the Adult, and be clear, precise, and aware (example: "I am depressed and I want to be cured of my illness through psychotherapy"), or it can be made with the Child, and, therefore, be confused and ambiguous and indicate objectives which are different from those which he really wants to reach ("I cannot stand it any more . . . help me . . .").

Often the underlying request is to cure someone else, something that occurs when the patient dwells persistently on the wrongs done to him by others and attributes to others the responsibility for his being unwell. When this happens, the patient comes to us with a Child who is scared and in need: "scared" because he is afraid of this new figure of the therapist and of the "strange things" which he can do; "in need" because, obviously, he is incapable of self-reliance.

One should be careful and not *collude* with this Child: do not make promises which cannot be kept; do not refute him, particularly if the contract is not valid, but confront him at the Adult level, giving him the message that you respect him *as a person*, even if you are not willing to work without a contract, given that he can, with help, change (*permission*).

Another thing to clarify in respect of the initial request is the difference between "understanding" and "changing": most people are motivated to want "to understand" why something is as it is, and this request should be confronted from the beginning because it needs to be made clear that *the objective of the therapy is change.*

The first interview and the formation of the therapeutic alliance. Alliance and pseudo-alliance

The basis of the *therapeutic alliance* is the first interview: often many psychological games are established and predetermined from the first interview.

The relationship between therapist and patient is often *pre-structured* from variables that precede the first interview. We can differentiate between *general precedents* and *specific precedents* (Novellino, Eric Berne Institute Seminars).

"*General precedents*" refers to the client's previous knowledge about the therapist, both personally (an old friend, a parent, etc.), and from the media (publicity or photo in the newspapers, reading a book by the therapist, knowing an ex-patient, etc.); these general precedents will determine the way in which the therapeutic alliance or a pseudo-alliance is formed.

"*Specific precedents*" have a more professional premise, which can be the referral of the patient to the therapist by his doctor, or the competence of a specific therapist regarding the pathology of the patient.

These precedents determine the extent to which the client comes to the therapist with preformed expectations about the therapy and the therapist, and, therefore, with fantasies, more or less magical, omnipotent, or depressive, which sooner or later should be analysed so as not to create, from the beginning, games which would inevitably lead to the interruption of the therapy. Therefore:

> all these precedents, fantasies, or games are the origin of that which is called the "preformed transference", which can be positive, negative, or ambivalent, based on the preceding experience of the patient.

Starting with the first interview, one should consider the possibility that there is already a preformed transference. When we explored the source of the referral of the patient, I emphasised that this is very important in order to investigate the motivation of the patient for seeking therapy.

When the source of the referral is doctors or other professional health workers, it is necessary to be careful: often the motivation to "do therapy" comes more from the person who makes the referral than from the person referred and the only reason that the patient comes is that he generates anxiety in the person making the referral (this is a very common game among neurologists who also take psychiatric patients into care, above all when the pharmacological therapy reaches its inevitable limits). "You need to have a chat with a psychologist . . ." is one of the most dismissive utterances a patient can hear in respect of both his problem and of the psychotherapy he starts. And the client sometimes repeats the sentence: "The doctor told me to come here to have a chat with you . . .".

Other sources of referral are often *institutions* (courts, schools, family, etc.); when this happens, it triggers something that is called the *"three-handed contract"*: it is advisable that in these cases the therapist clarifies with the institution what is expected of him, and this is particularly so when the institution making the referral is the family.

Another source of referral one should look into is that of the patient who goes through the process that I call the *"descent into hell"*. It can happen that a patient who initially goes to see an "important" therapist is sent, with whatever excuse, to a "less important" therapist, and so on. In such a case, the patient arrives with the feeling that he has been sent to someone who will not know how to really cure him, and, therefore, he will present a *negative preformed transference* regarding the therapist. Or the client has already "gone through" a certain number of professionals and arrives before us with a resigned sense of defeat (and great potential for persecuting behaviour).

Aims of the first interview

One should clarify that, by the "first" interview, one does not necessarily mean only the first session, but all the sessions that are required to arrive at least at the definition of the contract (*preliminary interviews*).

Essentially, the objectives that are important to reach in the first interview are:

I.	To explore the motivation of the patient to undertake therapy.
2.	To collect information/to know the patient.
3.	To give information about/to make known the way of working.
4.	To communicate to the patient the idea of the opportunity and the usefulness of therapy.
5.	To establish a setting and to define a therapeutic contract.

The motivation of the patient

The task of the therapist is that of verifying how much the patient is motivated by the therapy, and, in conditions of weak motivation, to verify what could be done to increase it. The variables to take into consideration are:

seriousness (of the clinical picture)	specific competence
motivation (to change)	motivation (to accept)
PATIENT	THERAPIST

Regarding the motivation of the patient, one should consider that in general the motivation for the treatment is tied to both phenomena of resistance and to the seriousness of the observed syndrome.

We usually have:

$$\text{motivation of the patient} = \frac{1}{\text{resistance}}$$

but also often:

$$\text{motivation of the patient} = \frac{1}{\text{seriousness}}$$

In connection with this, there is the interesting conceptualisation of the so-called "20% rule", which owes itself to the empirical studies of Woollams and Brown (1978).

The 20% rule refers to the division of a sample population of 100 patients, divisible in five bands.

This rule takes into account different possibilities of motivational relationships between patient and therapist, determined by factors pertaining to both components of the dyad, and which lead to five groups of potential "couplings".

The factors which pertain to the patient are:

1. The gravity of the pathology, both in a clinical sense and with reference to the level of functioning of the ego, to the capacity of insight, to the awareness of the self.
2. The motivation of the patient to change.

These two factors are often inversely proportional, so that the more seriously pathological patients are less motivated by the therapy.

The factors which are peculiar to the therapist are:

1. Competence.
2. The motivation of the therapist, or, rather, the interest that the therapist has in working with a particular patient in a particular moment.

The types of relationships that can be developed between patient and therapist vary between these two extremes of the continuum:

(a)   a patient with not too serious a pathology is very motivated by the therapy, which requires a therapist who is minimally competent and minimally motivated, who develops a simple work of channelling the energy of the patient and who, at least, does not harm him;

(b)   a patient with a very serious pathology and with a low motivation for the therapy, for whom a very competent and very motivated therapist is required.

In the latter situation, it is evident that a therapist who is not very competent but is very motivated (such as, typically, those who lean towards the role of Rescuer) would not serve the patient well; similarly, it would not serve to have a very competent therapist who had low motivation for the treatment.

This rule, although empirical, is very useful, above all in avoiding games at the beginning of the process, and implies, obviously, a careful analysis of the situation with particular attention to the gravity of the problems of the patient and to the therapist's own competence, motivations, and Adult "motives".

For there to be a high probability that the therapist starts from an Adult relationship instead of from the position of a game as a Rescuer, it is necessary to establish motives by making the patient part of the consideration of the various types of treatment the therapist can offer, and verifying that he has the time and the economic means to go into therapy; moreover, between motives and motivations, there must be "interest" and "curiosity", which are essential with regard to the patient. At the beginning of the activity, for example, a professional could have excessive economic needs, but this Adult "motive" can lead to his accepting a client in a non-selective way, to the detriment of the client, for whom he might not have real "competence" and experience: constant supervision of the cases can protect the setting from the beginning of the possible differences between the Adult motives, Adult competence, and Child motivation of the therapist.

By motivation of the therapist, I mean the urge to accept a patient: this can be constituted by interest, curiosity, or by the desire to help. A trap is triggered when the interest in the patient is directed to areas of pathology similar to those that are unresolved in ourselves or in loved ones (for example, the therapist has personal experience of a "depressed" mother): this, in fact, would lead to the magical fantasy of helping ourselves to resolve our problems, or even helping our own "depressed" mother, through helping the patient. This type of situation would need to be evaluated carefully through the analysis of preformed countertransference.

With regard to the desire to *help* (Adult level), which should be distinguished from the desire to *rescue*, the *key question* that one should ask oneself is: "What would happen to this person if I do not treat him?"

If the answer arrived at is that without us the patient does not have a hope, then, most probably, we are in a Rescuer role, since what is more likely is that the patient can be helped by other therapists.

Gathering of information

One should collect information, in the first place, about the *source of the referral*, asking the patient the classic questions about the why, the how, and who sent him to us; in the second place, one should ask questions about the history of the patient and about his current situation (reminiscent of a psycho-medical approach).

One should not underestimate this style of questioning because, from this, one can obtain much information about the script of the patient; a person who, at forty years of age, lives alone, who has many failures in love relationships, or who takes drugs, can reveal many things to us about his script.

It is good to ask questions also to reconstruct, in a longitudinal sense, the *development of the child*. Many useful elements come from knowing whether or not a person has always lived in the same environment: for example, children of military personnel, or of immigrants, who have never had a fixed residence during childhood and who, in consequence, might have assimilated the injunctions of "don't belong", "don't be part of", "don't be intimate". Furthermore, one should ask questions about the factual life of the person, always remembering that the therapist must improve the life of a person, not his intellectual quotient. All the information gathered will be translated later according to the terms of transactional analysis.

Another way to gather information is through *script question-naires*.

At the end of the information gathering, a question is included about the expectations of the patient in respect to the therapy.

Giving information

During the first interview, it is important that the therapist also gives information on:

(a) how the therapy functions;
(b) how long it might last;
(c) how the setting is structured.

Regarding the first point, remember that an important thing to say to the patient is that the therapy functions through *work carried out by two people*, that is, through a sharing of tasks and responsibility. One has to communicate clearly to the patient, above all to someone who displays magical expectations, that *one does not give advice* and there will be no intervening in practical life; the task of the therapist will be to *help him decide*, increasing his capacity for self-exploration with the aim of better self-determination.

Regarding the *length* of the therapy, the only plausible information is that the patient should know if he is facing a short therapy (in which case one can make a general forecast of between six months and one year); otherwise, it should be clarified that the temporal criteria is rather tied:

> • to the periodic checks regarding the reaching of the objectives;
> • to the attention owed to constructive use of the therapeutic time.

Finally, one should explain how, from a *setting* point of view, the therapy functions, and on this point one should be very clear from the start, in such a way that all possible future games regarding the setting are analysable.

I summarise the information that is necessary to provide about the setting:

I. How the intervention is structured in terms of time (= frequency of the meetings)

2. Length of the meetings, with the starting time and the ending time

3. If there is a fixed time and/or day, or if the date of the following meeting will be established each time (procedure to avoid if possible)

4. The cost, per session and monthly with modality of payment

5. What the rules are in case of a missed session: the principle is that the patient has the responsibility for payment, and possible exceptions should be agreed clearly and with well-founded motivation

6. It is advisable to inform the patient of periods for holiday breaks. In this regard, it would be opportune if the holiday period of the patient coincided with the holidays of the therapist, as this is very protective for him. In the case that it is not possible to make the two periods coincide, it is advisable to tell the patient in advance, so that he can prepare for the absence of the therapist, and possibly analyse with him his possible experiences of abandonment

7. It is useful to explain the rule about the interruption of the therapy by the patient before reaching the end of the contract. The patient who wants to interrupt the therapy before the end should be asked to talk about it to the therapist and, together with him, analyse it; furthermore, it is necessary that after this communication he commits to coming to therapy for a certain number of sessions established with the therapist.

Contract and probe interventions

Classically, the contract is to be done during the first interview; however, this rule is valid only for patients with a sufficiently functioning Adult. For patients who are confused or in acute crisis, the contract does not enter into the aims of the first interviews and should even be postponed until sufficient work of decontamination has been done.

By probe interventions, one means those exploratory interventions which some therapists already use during the first interview to study the reactions of the patient: these have both a diagnostic aim (based on the gathering of defences evoked from the stimulus: defences of low or high level? Do I have in front of me a marginal or a neurotic organisation?), and one of exploring the motivation.

The probe interventions of *interpretation* are classic. Nevertheless, with these interventions one should be *very careful*, because if, on the one hand, it is true that the patient needs to know how the therapist works, it is also true that, for the interventions to be successful, it is necessary that the therapeutic alliance be established. A probe inter-vention with a confrontation can be experienced as aggressive by a person with a narcissistic structure. Both interventions carry a certain amount of risk because, due to the change of pathology we witness (turning towards manifestations which are more and more marginal), the possibility of activating serially more than one defence mechanism of a low level is relevant (identification, introjection–projection, ideal-isation, splitting, omnipotence, negation).

It is useful to remember that in the first interviews, it is preferable to avoid crossing the levels of the games.

Example:

"Doctor, do you think that a person *like me* can succeed in getting cured?"

This displays the social level of the Adult and the psychological level of the Child, which communicates a self-discounting viewpoint, which can provide the stimulus to "do something for me" with which one could collude through an inadequate narcissistic desire for chal-lenge in the therapist.

We have two possible inadequate interventions by the therapist:

1. If the therapist replies: "I don't know. It is impossible to establish this at the beginning" (from the Adult), this will prematurely cross the psychological level, leaving the Child unheard, with the risk of a premature interruption.
2. If the therapist replies: "Look, if you follow me as one should, you *surely* can reach your objectives!" (from Parent to Child).

With the second reply, the therapist has been narcissistically hooked and, most probably, will achieve his pay-off at the expense of a disappointed and frustrated victim, while the patient will conclude that "no one can help me".

In essence, the therapist should *calibrate* his own reply, sending a double message to both the Adult and to the Child of the patient: "I think that you are a person with doubts about self-esteem, and if we go from here, we could work effectively and reach valid objectives for your life."

The reason for this caution is motivated by the fact that, all things considered, games are the best things that the patient has devised up to that moment to conserve his stock of strokings; they have a *defen-sive function* and constitute a social urge to safeguard at the beginning.

Prematurely crossing the levels of a transactional game means "discovering" the patient. It is more opportune in this phase to reply to both levels of the ulterior transaction of the patient. Taking the previous example:

Patient (Adult): "Can I succeed in getting cured?".
(Child): "A person who is not worth anything like me needs a great rescuer! Please, you do it!"
Therapist (Adult to Adult): "I consider that with the therapy you can achieve results."
(Adult to Child): "I will help you above all to acquire a sense of your worth!"

CHAPTER SIX

The therapeutic contract

Contract as content and as process

In his works, Berne defines the contract as *an explicit bilateral commitment for a course of defined action* (1966). Transactional analysis is, therefore, a method of psychotherapy with a *contractual* character, which places particular care and precision in analysing and classifying the various possible forms of therapeutic contract and the possible relative developments in the treatment of the patient.

When we speak of *contract*, the first important distinction to consider is that between contract understood as *content* and contract understood as *process* (Novellino, 1998). We will use the following definition (Novellino, Eric Berne Institute Seminars).

> Contract: agreement between patient and therapist on the AIMS and the HOW-TOS of the therapy.

Speaking of contract as content refers to the classic definition of the term (Berne's *professional contract*, 1966), that is, to the agreement between patient and therapist on the objectives of the therapy. The objective is to be proposed by the patient and accepted by the therapist, even if it is important to clarify that it is not necessary for the person to come to therapy with a contract already prepared. Identifying which is the current situation and which is the desired one, defining the problem and the consequent aim, is an important part of the contractual phase and of the therapy in general.

In the second case, that is to say, the contract understood as process, attention is focused on the relationship of *alliance* that is created between patient and therapist; therefore, on the reciprocal availability, to be verified at times during the course of the therapy, the type of relationship which one is experiencing, and the respective positions regarding the therapeutic aim.

In other words, the contract, at the level of process, consists of using the therapeutic alliance, including the transference and countertransference relationship, with the aim of reaching the therapeutic objective.

It is opportune to remember that a fundamental part of the success of a therapist is the restructuring of the patient–therapist relationship from Child–Parent to Adult–Adult.

The growth of a person in therapy is marked by the abandonment of the old modality of relationship with the therapist, characterised by magical expectations and by continuously seeking external support, and the installation, in its place, of a new type of relation, based on the recognition of the therapist as a person (not as a miracle-worker) and, therefore, on the reappropriation of one's own potential and capacity for self-reliance.

Administrative contract

Another side of the contract to take into consideration, with the aim of its correct evaluation, is the whole of the rules which characterise it as a professional type of relationship, and which goes under the name of *business contract* (Steiner, 1974) or *administrative contract* (Berne, 1966).

There are four criteria to respect so that patient and therapist can formulate a valid business contract:

1. *Mutual consent*: consists of a reciprocal agreement between patient and therapist about the aim of the therapy.

2. *Valid consideration*: concerns an effective exchange between the two parties, in which the therapist offers the professional capability and the patient the payment for this capability.

3. *Competence*: concerns both the parties, as the patient should have a capacity for Adult control of what he is doing and should be able to establish aims, while the therapist should make his professional and deontological validity available to that specific patient. The contract, therefore, would not be valid with persons who have an altered state of consciousness, either clinically or psychologically, or have mental insufficiency, or are psychotics in an acute phase, etc. The therapist should have professional competence, which includes theoretical–practical knowledge and the resolution, through personal therapy, of possibly serious intrapsychic and interpersonal problems.

4. *Legal object*: refers to the legality of the objective of the therapy, which must be within the terms of the current law and of the deontological code of the professional.

Soft and hard therapy contracts

The *therapy contracts* are those through which the *aim* of the therapy is established.

These can be differentiated as soft and hard contracts:

*   *soft contracts* concern the patient becoming aware, the cognitive comprehension of the problem ("I want to understand why ...". "I want to explore how ..." etc.)
*   *hard contracts* are instead concerned with a behavioural change ("I want to stop ..." or "I want to start ...").

During the psychotherapeutic treatment, one can use further specific forms of contract:

*   the *work contract*, for example, refers to the therapeutic aim for a well-defined situation in space and time: an individual session, a group, a marathon ("I want to work on ...");
*   *homework* consists of assignments of a behavioural nature which are considered useful for reaching the aim of the therapy or for maintaining it;

- *contracts of autonomy*: this means, instead, those contracts in which the aim of the therapy is not only and simply a behavioural change, but a change of the script of the person, therefore also aiming for a cognitive and emotive change, for which the therapy is not only at the symptomatic level, but is, rather, a restructuring of the personality
- the so-called *three-cornered contracts* (English, 1975) occur in situations in which the psychotherapy is not requested by the patient himself, but is commissioned by someone else: family, school, company, court.

These cases should be carefully evaluated by the therapist with regard to mutual consent, which, let us remember, is one of the most important elements for the validity of a contract of therapy. One should, therefore, take into account, in such cases, that the request does not come from the patient and, consequently, his motivational level is often very low, and the attitude in therapy can be characterised by defences such as evasiveness, aggressiveness, and compliance. Therefore, separating, during the first sessions, the patient's need and his own motivation from those of whoever sent him to therapy takes on great importance: for example,

"Well, we have seen the motives behind your being sent to therapy. But if you accept that you can gain benefits from the therapy, what would *you* like, now that we have established what the others would like?"

It is, moreover, essential that the therapist should reassure the patient that the things said in therapy will not be disclosed outside and that whatever the third party (the person who sent him) does, the therapist will never reveal such things.

- The *contracts of closing the script escape hatches* (Boyd, 1986; Holloway, 1974) concern very delicate points of psychotherapeutic treatment. The script escape hatches are those *actings out* that the Child ego state creates, during the construction of the script, when he thinks that going on in the future with the decisions taken could be too burdensome. In other terms, in the event that the solution devised by the Little Professor for survival becomes unsustainable, the person will take his own pathological tendencies to extreme consequences. To put it more analytically, the depressive type of personality will have *suicide* as an escape hatch, the paranoid type, *homicide,* and the one characterised by desperation, sense of impotence, fugue from others, will tend to *madness.*

> What one should do is quickly confront behaviours and tendencies which are self-harmful, even when these are sub-clinical. In the presence of behaviour (or of possible behaviour) which does not take into account the potential danger or risk to another, in the face of self-aggressiveness in all of its forms, and each time the situation runs the risk of becoming dangerous, one needs to stipulate an escape hatch contract with the client, for example: "I ask of you the commitment not to harm yourself (or not to do harm, or not to do foolish acts), whatever happens to you."

After the contract has been made, one will work in therapy on the underlying problem. In the case of *contracts of non-suicide and non-homicide, of non-violence towards you and/or others,* the *written and signed contract* is useful: attention should be given to the expiry times of the proposed commitments (expiry times should be short and renewable), and to incomplete and "scholastic" signatures (first the surname and then the given name), since such things reveal a Negative Compliant AC which intends to transgress. Sometimes, the text "I commit myself not to hurt myself voluntarily or involuntarily from today until . . ." can be stated more directly: "I will not hurt myself voluntarily or involuntarily from today until . . ."

There is another instance in which the contract of therapy is not stipulated voluntarily by the patient: it is when there is a contract with patients with a non-functioning Adult. Here, obviously, the unwillingness derives from the fact that the person does not have, at that moment, an Adult capable of accepting the contract, as it is too confused: for example, a person in an acute psychotic crisis. In these situations, the importance of the therapist taking into account different factors before entering into a relationship of therapy is shown very clearly. It presents the opportunity to evaluate one's own availability to commit oneself, to invest energy, and to have the support of external structures, etc.

Schiff (1975) strongly advises against individual therapy with very seriously depressed patients and, in general, with serious psychotics. It is advisable to send such patients to someone who practises within a firm framework, to collaborate with psychiatrists, or to use as a therapeutic coadjuvant a residential option (for example, a community) that provides both protection and gratification to the individual within a rigorous setting.

Unacceptable contracts

"Non-acceptable" contracts (Goulding & Goulding, 1979) are:

(a) *Parent contracts*: in which the objective of the therapy is dictated mainly by norms: "I must try to stop smoking"
(b) *contracts to change others*: taken more often than not from a position of "Rebellious Child", it is, therefore, within the script. Example: a woman enters into therapy to change her husband who is a gambler
(c) *contracts of psychological games*: through which the Child of the patient proposes himself for therapy to confirm something about himself, others, and life, using the therapist as a means to this end. Example: "Doctor, I am here to try to understand if people like me can change!" (game: "Now I've got you, you son of a bitch").

Therapy without a contract

There are situations in which persons who have a well-defined contract can experience, during the therapy, a very emotional situation, whose content might not correspond to that of the initial contract.

Even if there is not a related or specific contract in these cases, it is possible to intervene.

Another situation in which one can—in fact, one absolutely should—conduct therapy without a contract is that in which the patient is manifesting harmful or self-destructive behaviour dictated by the script: for example, he is hurting himself, or he is attacking someone, etc.

Finally, one can work without a contract with persons who, at the beginning of the therapy, do not have a well-defined aim, but are nevertheless showing significant signs that there is an opportunity for intervention and, later, to be able to agree a contract.

Holloway's contract

Holloway (1974), one of the first heirs of Berne, proposed a technical modality to help the patient formulate a valid therapeutic contract, which involves writing it in four different areas (graphically, it is suggested that the page should be divided into four cross-directional sectors):

- what is the *problem* that I intend to resolve with the therapy;
- what is the *aim* that I intend to reach:
- what is the *change* that I should pursue;
- what is the *obstacle* that can prevent the change.

PROBLEM   AIM

⇧

⇦   ⇨

⇩

CHANGE   OBSTACLE

Let us examine a clinical example.

G is a middle-aged man, who asks to undergo therapy because of a reactive depressed state following a great disappointment at work. His expectations are magical, in the sense that he expects he will be cured by the simple fact of having "some meetings". The therapist explains to him that the efficacy of the work will depend on establishing a working alliance, with a reciprocal commitment, and he proposes to start from a well-defined contract. To this end, he helps the patient to formulate the contract, using the method outlined by Holloway. G proposes to work on it at home, and in the following session, the patient reads what he has written:

- *problem*: "I feel depressed";
- *aim*: "to be cured of the depression";
- *change*: "to return to being myself";
- *obstacle*: [none].

The therapist comments on the work done, helps G to specify the different areas in a more constructive way, and at the end, after decontamination work, the result is the following:

- *problem*: "I remain passive in the face of a disappointment";
- *aim*: "to take up initiatives again and try to find support from others";
- *change*: "bring out the hidden anger and the distrust in me and in others";
- *obstacle*: "delegating everything to the therapist".

CHAPTER SEVEN

The Bernean methodology

The classic Bernean methodology: the therapeutic themes

The transactional analysis literature presents a series of themes expressed by Berne, half-way between methodology and philosophy (1966). These underline the general attitude that the transactional analyst must have, so that the techniques that he uses may be effective.

The Bernean theme that emerges is that of the *patient as a real person*.

In all of the works of Berne, considering the patient as a "person" is highlighted as important, and this implies a concept of responsibility of the patient. The patient constructed his script by himself; he did it for motives which were surely valid at the moment of the script decision, and precisely because of this he has the responsibility and the power to reconstruct himself with the help of the therapist.

Berne (1966) draws attention to the situation of a frequent game, which is described like this: a patient, after having different experiences of analytic therapy, presents himself to the transactional analyst with a precise manifestation. He has an Adapted Child, camouflaged by an Adult (pseudo Adult); the Adapted Child has learnt psychiatric language and uses psychoanalytic jargon; his main defence mechanism is rationalisation; he tends to respond to everything the therapist proposes to him with "already said", and "already known". In reality, what happens is that the Child of the patient is playing, at a deeper level, something that in Martian language (Berne, 1972) is translated as "fleece someone else", or "fool someone else". What the patient does, with his Little Professor, is to study the field to ascertain whether he is faced with a parent different from the previous ones, and, to be able to trust him, he investigates whether this "parent" will do something which the others were not capable of offering him. Therefore, the more frequent the patient's experiences of previous therapy were, the more resolute the analyst must be in this game.

Berne asserts that if the game is not confronted and analysed quickly, it is tantamount to consenting to the patient's wish that the therapist should "fleece someone else". The lengthier the previous therapy was, or the more therapists the patient had consulted, the earlier the Child of the patient will arrive at the conclusion that "this one is just the same as the others". On the surface, the patient will be seeking the rewards of triumph, but, at a more profound level, there will be a reaction of despair in the Child.

Berne introduces, at this point, an important concept called "the balance of the game". This states that the therapist should maintain a sense of balance, so as not to confront the game either too soon or too late. If he does it too soon, that is, before establishing a therapeutic alliance and before having reinforced the Adult of the patient, he takes away from the latter some of his "known" strokes. If the game is confronted too late, when the "escalation" is beginning to move towards abandonment of the therapy and, therefore, becoming a repetition of the previous therapeutic relationships, the therapist is experienced as a "Victim" ("I have trapped him as well"), and the Child of the patient enters into a situation in which he no longer expects the therapist to be a different parent.

This is a neurotic type of situation in which the person, to defend himself from his own internal Persecutor, projects his psychological role of Victim externally in order to feel less anxious; in this case, if the therapist confronts the game too soon, he prevents the patient from defending himself; if he confronts it too late, the projection is effective, and the therapist has become "a victim" like the previous therapists.

Berne suggests using the following ways of approach:

- *use extremely simple language.* If the patient says, for example, "I have to resolve an Oedipal conflict", one should reply: "What is it that you really mean? In reality, how are things with your wife?"
- *do not accept the patient's use of other labels.* For example: "You know, I come here because they have diagnosed me with a narcissistic personality with paranoid defences." Accepting this type of "reasoning", the therapist swallows the patient's persecution whole. One should, therefore, reply in the following way: "That is what they told you, but in fact, what do you really think about yourself?"
- *do not accept the patient's use, in referring to himself, of terms such as "immature" and "childish".* Example: "I realise that sometimes I argue with my wife and my immaturity is really quite disgraceful, other times . . .". In this case, it is advisable to resituate the self-diagnosis of the patient in a positive way: "I think that that which you define immature is an attempt by your Child part to communicate that . . ."

Berne wrote that the patient should realise that his Child ego state is present and has a right to be heard. The client has to understand that he is not at all infantile and immature—in the derogatory sense of these terms—but, rather, has a confused Child ego state, and underneath this confusion there is the potential of the attractiveness and spontaneity of a real child.

The *second theme* is a slogan, which consists of *changing and not improving*. The slogan of the therapy of improvement ("I made much progress") is: "You can't be better until you are completely analysed", that is, all the motives are understood. The slogan of the therapy of change (or cure) is: "First try to be well and change; then, if it still interests you, we will analyse why".

The *third theme* deals with the phenomenon of the "real doctor" who "cures". We have three suggestions by Berne on this point:

- do not harm
- stroke the areas of health
- help nature take its course.

In accordance with the *fourth theme*, the therapy, once the contractual base is set up, is a specification to cure rather than to improve.

Berne asserts that a contract, to be valid, should be clear to a five-year-old child (that is, expressed in terms comprehensible to a child).

Within a contract, Berne specifies the *contractual rules of a group* (1966):

- the time of the start of the sessions should be clearly established at the beginning of a relationship. Example: "the group starts Thursday at . . . o'clock", etc.; this is in the interests of the time structure of the activity, and is useful in highlighting games about the time (e.g., arriving early, arriving late, leaving early, etc.);
- it is important to clearly establish the modality of payment for the sessions;
- it should be clear that it is permissible to say anything, without any exception;
- whatever is said should remain in the group (principle of discretion);
- any putting into action is to be excluded: no sex, no physical aggression.

The *fifth theme* concerns the so-called *here-and-now*. The purpose of the modality of the transactional analyst leading the group is to analyse the ego states, the transactions, the games, and the manifestations of the script as they come up in the group *environment*.

In the *sixth theme*, it is affirmed that psychotherapy with transactional analysis assumes that the transactional analyst, as a way of interpreting what happens, identifies:

(a)   the ego states (structural analysis);
(b)   the transactions (transactional analysis proper);
(c)   games and antitheses (analysis of the games);
(d)   script and permissions (script analysis).

The phases of therapy according to Berne

The *phases of the therapy* according to Berne (1966) are:

(a)   decontamination (structural analysis);
(b)   recathexis;
(c)   clarification;
(d)   reorientation;
(e)   cognitive–emotional integration;
(f)   expression.

Decontamination

The patient's Adult is to be separated from the borders existing between Parent and Child; or, rather, phenomenologically the person realises that what he has experienced as an Adult is, instead, exteropsychic or archeopsychic content. The dynamic result of the decontamination should be a recathexis of the Adult.

One of the ways to verify that a decontamination has taken place is to note whether the patient uses the Adult more often when he is in situations that he finds difficult. This will show whether or not the egogram (which derives from functional analysis: Normative Parent, Affective Parent, Adult, Free Child, Adapted Child) has been modified.

Recathexis (rebalancing of energy)

Recathexis is re-energising: once the Adult of the patient is decontaminated, the energy flux will be orientated towards the functioning of the Adult and the Free Child.

Clarification

The patient acquires the capacity to comprehend what was told to him and is capable of maintaining the structural condition of a decontaminated Adult. He understands, for example, that previously he was playing a psychological game and, consequently, he will effect the reorientation towards an awareness of a new behavioural option.

Reorientation

The patient reorientates his own behaviour: he has understood the game he played, and becomes capable of putting into action new behaviours.

Cognitive–emotional integration

At the cognitive level, thinking is separated from intellectualising and from rationalising. The patient goes from a defensive use of his Adult to a constructive use of it, which is to say that he "thinks" to resolve his problem. At the affective level, the emotional activity is separated, to distinguish natural emotion from racket emotion. At this point, the thinking is integrated with the natural emotions, the person will feel an emotion tied to the problem, and will think about the solutions to get rid of it. The final result of this process is that which Berne defines as the "direct line", understood as the expression of the affection which concerns the here-and-now. We can, in general terms, define the whole as a "recovery of spontaneity". It is to be understood as an emotional expression correlated to the reality of the here-and-now.

Expression

This refers to the direct expression of the emotions in the here-and-now: the person has realised his capacity for intimacy.

Bernean tactics of intervention on the Adult

The material that Berne proposes in *Principles of Group Therapy* (1966) for the analytic–transactional methodology concerns the so-called *therapeutic operations* (a semantic equivalent of the terms: *techniques* and *tactics*).

The ego state "target" is considered to be the Adult.

To be able to correctly set up the comprehension and the use of the Bernean operations, one is to take the following into account:

(a)   what Berne means by the Adult ego state. The latter has been "popularised" by some authors (see Harris, 1971) as a sort of computer. Berne, in fact, emphasised that part of the explicit functionality of the Adult ego state is comparable, by analogy, to a computer. In reality, the Adult ego state is within the general definition of what an ego state is: a set of thoughts, feelings, and behaviours. Therefore, when we speak of recovering the Adult ego state (in other words, of decontamination), one should understand the Adult not as a computer, but, rather, as a system which is integrated and correlated to the here-and-now of cognitive and intellectual capacity and that of affection;

(b)   Berne developed his own methodological theory, but, unfortunately, his premature death occurred before he could completely develop his work. He made it clear in his works that the point to which he had brought the methodology of transactional analysis (decontamination) was only a part of the approach. The regressive analysis that Berne illustrates for the Child represents his first attempt to lead the transactional methodology beyond decontamination towards a deconfusion of the Child, understood not only in a cognitive sense, but also in an emotional one. Berne then left this matter outstanding, which meant that the tactics devoted to deconfusion were reserved for operations of the cognitive–psychodynamic type.

So, how much did Berne leave us about the techniques of the transactional analysis method?

Let us look at the various operations in detail.

Bernean therapeutic operations

On the Adult:
interrogation;
specification;
confrontation;
explanation;
illustration;
confirmation;
interpretation;
crystallisation:
- from I to 4 develops a realignment of the borders;
- 5 and 6 reinforce the limits (interventions of interposition);
- 7 and 8 are specific to deconfusion.

With the Parent:
support;
reassurance;
persuasion;
exhortation;
permission.

On the Child:
(I) regression analysis.

Interrogation

This is the first therapeutic operation and consists of a question posed by the Adult of the therapist to the Adult of the patient.

The therapist uses a question to solicit and make explicit the content that can be clinically decisive for clarifying and resolving the contract. The example which Berne gives is the following: "In essence, your husband really hit you?"

The questions have to be clear and explicit, clinically relevant; in the example quoted, the question serves to make clear whether or not there is a psychological game of the third degree. Therefore, it can be clinically decisive to perceive if a patient, in the game of "Uproar" or "Rapo", or even "Kick me", is playing a game of the first or the third degree. The intervention should be made through an Adult–Adult transaction; what can happen is that the patient could redefine the question, not answering with the Adult, but with the Parent. Berne suggests that the person could evade it by using prejudice, or dogmas. He could even redefine it with the Child, therefore complaining, excusing himself, asking for compassion, etc.

Berne suggests a series of precautions:

- use interrogation when there is a reasonable chance that the answer will be given with the Adult;
- therefore, do not ask questions when the person is agitated and there is a reasonable chance that he will not answer with his Adult, but that he will answer with the Parent or with the Child;
- if a patient is in a moment of despair, it is not the time to use interrogation, because he will answer with the Child;
- do not ask an excessive number of questions, but only those that are indispensable for the therapist's understanding of the content, otherwise he runs the risk of playing a game of "Psychiatry".

The therapist will have confirmation of a successful interrogation when he stimulates the Adult ego state in the patient.

In the final analysis, interrogation should *not* be used:

- when there is a likelihood that the patient will not answer with the Adult;
- if the Parent or the Child becomes activated;
- when one runs the risk of playing the game "Psychiatry";
- when the question already contains the answer.

Specification

This is an operation which consists of a statement by the therapist which confirms information obtained through a previous interrogation; the aim is that of returning to this in a subsequent phase. Therefore, to return to the example already cited of the husband who hits his wife, when the therapist hears: "Yes, my husband hits me", he can reply with: "Therefore, when you argue and your husband hits you, what happens is that you tolerate the situation, which repeats itself over and over again."

The specification is used when one thinks that the patient might subsequently deny an important content (as can occur in a hysterical personality, which tends to remove any unpleasant content).

Something that was not really said by the patient is not to be specified, otherwise one runs the risk of playing "Psychiatry of the psychoanalytic type" and it would end with proposing, in the deconfusion phase, a mistaken interpretation, because it is founded on a presumed fact. Making an interpretation signifies giving back to the patient decodified material that he has previously provided.

Confrontation

This is the intervention in which the therapist uses a piece of information previously obtained from the patient (and reinforced with a specification), to highlight an incongruity. When the patient says: "I don't have any problem", it is the child, in this case, who is exchanged for the adult.

The adult of the therapist, using a piece of information already specified, crosses the transaction and confronts the incongruity, saying, "Although you say this now, in the last session you told me you felt very depressed."

This is a classic clinical situation in which the group is important, because it can confirm the previous words of the patient: this can even be something that confirms the good functioning of the group.

One uses confrontation:

- when the patient is playing "Stupid";
- when the patient cannot recognise, by himself, the incongruity.

One does *not* use confrontation:

- when the confrontation makes us feel cleverer and more intelligent than the patient.

In this specific case, Berne means that when the therapist realises, during an intervention, that he feels a negative countertransference, for example, a feeling of revenge or triumph, one should not use confrontation, which is not to be confused with the game "Now I've got you, you son of a bitch", or with the game "Blemish".

There is a link between interrogation, specification, and confrontation. In fact, if the confrontation is effective, this will be a signal that the specification was also congruous, and, consequently, the interrogation was carried out in a precise way.

The Bernean confrontation, which is an Adult–Adult transaction, differs from that of Schiff (1975), who works with psychotics who can become violent: with them, the transactions must be Parent–Child.

As in the *Bernean confrontation* the transaction is Adult–Adult, in this, two pieces of discordant information are confronted. In the *Schiffian confrontation*, instead, there is a confrontation between the Parent of the therapist and the confused Child of the patient, in which what is confronted is the passive behaviour: "Now stop getting agitated like that and think about what is happening".

Confrontation

1. Berne: Adult–Adult.
2. Schiff: Parent–Child.

Explanation

This consists of an attempt to energise, decontaminate, or reorientate the Adult of the patient: "At this moment you are starting a game of . . ." Or: "The ego state that you are using . . ."

In other words, this operation calls for the categorising, in transactional analysis terms, of a certain behaviour or attitude or dynamic of the patient: analysis of the ego states and of the transactions, analysis of psychological games, and cognitive analysis of the psychological script.

The therapist must be careful not to fall into the game of "Psychiatry of the transactional analysis type". The explanation is not to be confused with the interpretation, as it does not touch the archaic origin of the manifestations of the patient.

Illustration

This consists of an anecdote, or an exemplification, or even a meta-phorical explanation, which follows a fully successful confrontation. The anecdote has the aim of reinforcing the confrontation and soften-ing its possible negative effects.

Example: following a piece of information obtained through the interrogation of a patient who repeatedly got himself dismissed from work, the therapist specifies that the patient continually gets himself immersed in a series of problems. At this point, he follows the denial of the patient, who affirms that he does not have problems, even if he is always losing his job.

The therapist now intervenes, explaining to the patient that he is playing a game, at the end of which he will find his script of "rebel-lious victim" reinforced, and, therefore, the therapist can offer the patient a metaphorical reinforcement (in some way symbolic of the confrontation), saying, for example, "You behave in a similar way to the proverb which says: 'If you take the pitcher too often to the well, it will finally break'."

Another way to illustrate is that of telling a story in which one pro-poses again to the Child of the patient the same content which was proposed to the Adult, but using themes that are more analogous and therefore less menacing in order to reinforce and soften it. One can, for example, tell a story which apparently refers to another person: "There once was a patient who repeatedly ... Do you want to know how it finished?"

As an alternative, one can also tell a fable. In practice, it is advis-able to use a modality that tells the Child of the patient (metaphori-cally or symbolically) that which was previously affirmed with the Adult and which, if it remained the same, would scare the Child. The anecdote or the illustration, which should also contain humour, should be used when it is certain that there is a connection between explanation and illustration for the patient; that is, when the confron-tation is still active.

The illustration should not be used:

- when the Child does not emerge easily and the Parent of the patient appears strong or lacking in imagination;
- when one can, predictably, provoke a parental criticism: for example: "Well then, he is not a serious person!"

All of the interventions, up to the confirmation (see below), are interventions that have decontamination and the re-equilibration of energy as the primary objective. Nevertheless, the illustration (like the confirmation) is an intervention that has, more than anything else, the value of reinforcing the decontamination; Berne calls them interventions of interposition.

The first four interventions have the aim of restructuring, of decontaminating, the situation of the Adult. The illustration and the confirmation aim to solidify the borders between Adult, Parent, and Child.

Confirmation

This is the operation through which the therapist reinforces the functioning of the Adult of the patient by revealing new material of confirmation presented by the patient, subsequent to the confrontation and to the illustration.

To return to the example of the patient who is always getting himself dismissed from his job, after he has been confronted and given an explanation of what he said (that is, his loser's script), it emerges that the patient not only gets himself sacked, but also gets rejected by women. When this material has emerged, the therapist adds it to what was previously said and explains to the patient that what happens to him with women is exactly what happens at work, because this is also a way to pursue his loser's script.

This is an operation to use when the Adult of the patient is sufficiently reinforced: therefore, only after decontamination.

Confirmation is *not* used:

● when the previous confrontation and illustration have been ineffective.

Interpretation

This is an operation whose aim is to deconfuse the Child by a re-codification of the past experience of the patient. On this point, Berne (1966) writes that while the first six operations have as an objective the clarification and the reinforcement of the Adult in a way that provides the therapist with an objective ego state to which he can turn, the aim of the interpretation is to resolve the conflict fixed in the Child. It is opportune, at this point, to recall that in the Bernean concept of the ego states, they are not "roles", but "states of experience", so that being in the Parent ego state does not mean "acting like" a parent, but being in a phenomenological and behavioural state derived from introjected models. When Berne sets up the therapeutic plan, he considers the ego states as different and separate entities. He uses a mathematical metaphor to describe the energetic situation or the therapeutic relationship. At the beginning of the therapy, the Adult of the therapist is present "against" the Parent and the Child of the patient, at least for those areas that are tied to the conflict. After decontamination, it will be the Adult of the therapist which collaborates with the Adult of the patient, and that is equivalent to a position of equilibrium. After the conflict is resolved, or, better, after the patient is deconfused, he will have a Child who has re-decided. The therapist will have on his side not only the Adult, but also a Child, and can, therefore, get the upper hand over the Parent of the patient. The position of the therapist will, therefore, be the following: he, with his Adult, works on three ego states of the patient which, before being decontaminated, were "confused" and, therefore, "in the problem", and were in conflict with the Adult of the therapist. After the decontamination, there will be both the Adult of the therapist and the Adult of the patient, who work in alliance on the conflict present between the Child and the Parent of the patient.

Decontamination is, consequently, the basis for arriving at a re-decision and reaching intrapsychic equilibrium.

In the deconfusion, we have the Adult of the therapist allied with the Adult and the Child of the patient, who will now have sufficient energy to overcome the script messages of the Parent.

Taking once more as an example the situation of the patient who gets himself dismissed, we can see which are the phases of therapeutic work linked to the Bernean operations. This patient, following the interrogations, provides the information that he lost his job; this information is then specified. The therapist then confronts it: if, for example, the patient says that even if he did lose his job he feels just as well as before, we can see that we are facing an incongruity. The therapist will subsequently intervene with the explanation, saying, "At this moment, you are playing a familiar game whose aim is to confirm your script of rebellious failure."

With the illustration, the therapist will intervene, providing a story with a metaphorical content: "Your emotional attitude reminds me of certain people who, because of a neurological disturbance, do not remember bleeding, they do not feel pain."

With the confirmation, he will pursue the speech, saying, "The fact that your amorous relationships end abruptly in a negative way is also a predictable result for a personality with a script of failure; in a sense, they are the same as getting yourself laid off."

With the interpretation, the therapist will affirm, "You have put yourself in the position of rebellious failure and you are still trying to attract the attention of your mother, trying to provoke compassion in her. The exact same thing happened when you wanted, in your fantasy, to take your mother's attention away from your father."

If this interpretation is refuted by the patient, it means:

- that there is error in the content; which means that in the explanation of the story of the anamnesis, of the historical and phenomenological analysis, there was no point of contact with the real experience of the patient;
- that it was premature. The client can, for example, say, "What does my mother have to do with the fact that I lost my job?"

If, previously, during the script analysis and/or during the regressive work, it emerged that the patient, in his relationship with his mother, had a tendency to place himself in the position of Victim with his Adapted Child, then the strategic consequence will be that the therapist can and should clarify that the patient now acts as a Victim at work and with women, just as he placed himself in the position of Victim with his mother. Consequently, the situations, even if they do not appear to be connected, have an analogous reference for the Child. In fact, losing a job, losing amorous relationships, "getting himself kicked" (for example, by the group), are distorted ways for the Child to repropose an old *Gestalt*. This operation is an interpretation: the therapist puts together the facts; he "cross-connects" them.

According to Berne, that which is pursued up until the "confirmation" is social control; the roots of the symptom remain, however, as the conflict remains; the Adult needs to be reinforced in such a way that it is capable of controlling the symptom.

Interpretation is the step that provides the opportunity to obtain deconfusion. To deconfuse clarifies to the patient that that which he is doing, in the here-and-now, is an attempt to close an old *Gestalt*.

Interpretation is used only when one is sure that the Adult of the patient is allied with the Adult of the therapist.

One needs to be careful not to slip from interpretation to intellectualisation (game of "Psychiatry").

Therefore, if the interpretation is shared with the patient, this often means that:

- this was erroneous, in that it does not correspond to the facts expected by the patient
- it is a premature interpretation because it indicates that the Adult of the patient is not listening.

The *positive or negative feedback* to the interpretation is not to be inferred simply with an affirmation or with a denial (Novellino, 1984b, 1998). The patient could also say, "Yes, it is like that", while the content does not correspond to reality: it would be a yes of compliance or of rationalisation.

We can ascertain whether this approval is real by observing that which the patient will express in what follows: it will be the subsequent behaviour and the following clinical material which indicate how the therapy is going and, therefore, if the interpretation was adequate. If, five minutes later, or in the subsequent session, the same things continue to be turned over in one's mind, the therapy stagnates even if the patient said, "Yes, it is like that": probably that proposal of the therapist was not the exact interpretation. If instead, the patient said, "No, it is not like that", and then freely lets dreams and other material emerge, this indicates that the interpretation was exact, but it still has to be emotionally accepted.

Crystallisation

This is an affirmation by the therapist applied to the Adult of the patient on the existential position in which the latter finds himself after the interpretation: he has the option of continuing to follow his decision of the script or to change it, moving towards autonomy.

The therapist, for example, says, "So what you did until now is to live the present in an attempt to resolve a past situation connected to your mother. Until now, you have experienced work relationships, amorous relationships, etc. as if you were interacting with your mother."

Berne maintains that during crystallisation the therapist should interfere as little as possible, be as little parental as possible; it must be the Adult of the patient, at that point, which decides. The contract has ended when, reciprocally, it is agreed that the desired change has been put into action. Crystallisation does not necessarily coincide with the end of the therapy; on the contrary, it is the point at which the Adult of the patient realises that from that moment on, he can change, that is, he no longer needs to resolve something which pertains to the past and instead can "be" in the present.

After the first six operations, the therapist has three options: he can

- crystallise the decontamination, which offers immediate symptomatic relief, and therefore stabilises social control;
- interpret;
- crystallise before reinforcing the decontamination, then follow with the interpretation.

Tactics of intervention with the Parent

Berne describes them as exceptional interventions aimed to back up the situation of the patient in moments of crisis: they do not have the aim of restructuring, but of sustaining.

There are four: support, reassurance, persuasion, and exhortation.

What the therapist uses for the four interventions indicated above is a Parent that is to be directed in the neo-psyche; therefore, it is aware of the role of the task.

The Parent interventions are used by the therapist when he finds himself facing an emergency situation and, more usually, when the Child of the patient is particularly anxious, confused, or agitated and threatens to *act out*.

Support is used by the therapist in moments of the therapy that are rather delicate: it does not help towards reaching comprehension, but it is a momentary "anxiety reliever" that allows the alliance to be maintained and to repropose the restructuring work when the Child of the patient is less scared, less anxious:

"Come on!"

Reassurance can consist of a sentence such as: "I think that what you are experiencing now is normal, it has occurred often at this stage of the therapy."

Persuasion can be achieved with a sentence of the type: "Don't you think that now that you feel blocked and you cannot think, it would be a good idea to breathe deeply, close your eyes . . ."

Exhortation can be expressed, for example, by "For me it is important that you continue to do therapy, to understand what happens."

The patient, becoming aware of the anxious material that is in him, could refuse to continue. The therapist should then follow by saying, "I think it is particularly important that you continue; I think that if you stop now, the consequences would be that you will head directly towards big problems."

In the work with the Parent, there is *also a fifth* intervention: *permission*, which is given by a transaction in which the therapist authorises, with his Parent, the Child of the patient to disobey the script injunction. Permission is given during a work of re-decision. It should be said that this is one of the aspects of Berne's work that has remained in an embryonic stage.

Tactics of intervention on the Child: regression analysis

Berne (1961) proposes that *regression analysis* is work specifically on the Child; this falls within the work of deconfusion. The technique consists of inviting the patient to lie down on the couch, after having explained to him the gist of the work he will do, and guiding him to go back to feel the child he has been, interacting with him as if he were really that child.

It is one of the areas that Berne did not develop, but that has become, subsequently, an important root of two other methodological approaches to deconfusion:

in the redecisional therapy of the Gouldings;
in the psychodynamic approach, with the revalorisation of the targeted use of the couch in the individual setting (Novellino, 2004).

CHAPTER EIGHT

Post-Bernean re-decision tactics

Impasses and re-decisions

I n the 1970s, thanks to the integration of transactional analysis and Gestalt therapy (Goulding & Goulding, 1976, 1979), the first alternative to the Bernean interpretation for developing a deconfusion was conceived.

Re-decision therapy, as a system of techniques, is based on a specific conceptual model: the theory of *impasse*.

Impasse is a term taken from Gestalt therapy and means to be blocked, to be at a point in which the resistance of the patient to change blocks the therapeutic process; the impasse is experienced as an internal conflict, in which a person can feel "confused, uneasy, strange", etc.

Robert and Mary Goulding theorised the existence of three possible impasses.

Theory of impasses (Goulding & Goulding)

First type: between P2 and A I.
Second type: between P I and A I.
Third type: between AC and FC.

- *Impasse of the first type* consists of a conflict between a counter-script message of P2 (for example *"Work hard"*) and a contrasting need of A1 (*"I want to relax"*); the intrapsychic relationship is I–You.
- *Impasse of the second type* occurs between an injunction of P1 (*"Do not exist"*) and a need of the child in A1 (*"I want to live"*); the relationship is I–You.
- *Impasse of the third type* is a conflict between the AC and a repressed FC (example: *"I would like to have success with women but I am shy"*); the relationship is I–I.

Impasse is, therefore, a conflict which occurs between a script message and a legitimate need: between a contaminated area and a healthy one; it is intra-egoic and it is more probable that it manifests itself in therapy before the progression to increasing messages of permission that create a contrast with the messages of the script.

Impasses and the developmental line. Neurosis of transference

In addition to the Gouldings, the theory of impasses has been studied by other transactional analysts. Ken Mellor, who collaborated for a long time with Schiff, provided a very important contribution in regard to the organisation of the personality by considering impasses from a developmental point of view (1975), so much so that he speaks of *degree* and not *type*.

According to Mellor, the *impasses* of the *first degree*, being replies to counter-script messages, are developed in a period in which the child is old enough to understand language (between the fourth and the eighth year); the *impasses* of the *second degree* are related to injunctions, that is, to messages given in mainly extra-verbal form, so that one absorbs them between the second and fourth year. It appears that the origin of *impasses* of the *third degree* can start in the first year of life and maybe even in the prenatal period.

The three types of *impasses* also correspond to three different phases of development in the capacity of learning (Table 5).

In relationships of parental poles expressed and projected in the three types of impasses (P2–P1–P0), different projections based on the moment of fixation of the impasse are verified (Novellino, 1985b, 1987): in this way, there will be a *cognitive transference* (P2 projected on the therapist), an *affective transference* (P1 projected), and a *somatic transference* (P0 projected).

Table 5. The correspondence between the three types of impasses and three different phases of development.

Impasses (Mellor)	Age	Structural level	Operational and decisional level of learning
First type (P2–C2)	4–8 years	1st order	A2
Second type (P1–C1)	2–4	2nd order	A1
Third type (P0–C0)	0–1	3rd order	A0

By transference neurosis, I mean:

> "that clinical situation characterised by the fact that the patient relives the original impasse in its full emotional intensity, experiencing the therapy unconsciously as if it were a parental pole of the impasse itself."

The seven components of re-decisional therapy

McNeel (1977) illustrated, following experimental research on the work of the Gouldings during intensive group marathons, that which he calls the seven components which make the re-decisional approach effective. I summarise them in the order indicated by the author:

- *emphasis on power and personal responsibility*: it is sustained by confrontations with the patient who delegates his own responsibility and power to third parties ("It makes me feel . . .") through a magic thought ("It always happens that . . ."), resorting to a supposition of inadequacy ("I try to . . .");
- *sustaining a nutritive environment*: by the targeted use of positive strokings and of humour which the child understands;
- use of a positive model of the leader;
- *separating the myth from reality*, for example, the expectation that someone else changes;
- *confrontation of the incongruities*, both verbal and non-verbal;
- *particular techniques*: analysis of psychological games, technique of the two chairs, say goodbye to the past, use of guided fantasies
- *procedural rules*: respect of the time limits, no to gossip in the group, prohibition of violence and sex during the groups.

Re-decision therapy: the two-chairs work

Options for the technique of the two chairs

Create an old scene (Goulding, 1972; Goulding & Goulding, 1976, 1979)
Disconnecting rubberbands (Erskine, 1974; Kupfer & Haimowitz, 1970).

The development of the re-decisional technique can start from two options. In the first option, the patient is guided to enter into an *archaic scene* in which he feels blocked emotions at the moment that the script was decided (Goulding & Goulding, 1979).

In the second option, one works from a racket emotion felt spontaneously in the here-and-now: *rubberband* (Erskine, 1974).

In the case of guided searching for *an archaic scene*, the process of taking the patient back to the re-decision follows a series of essential steps. Here are the ten steps of the re-decisional intervention, as described by Moiso (Institute for Transactional Analysis Seminars):

- relaxing the patient and protecting him from environmental and group interferences;
- expression in the present of the *current* situation which the script problem reproposes;
- amplified expression of the present emotions in that situation and becoming conscious of the decision of the script;
- reliving, through the amplification of the emotions, the *current* situation and the *original* one in which the decision was taken;
- awareness of the identity of the two decisions or, at any rate, of the sequence of the two decisions: that the one of today derives from the one of yesterday (compulsive repetition of the decision);
- expression of the emotions felt at the moment of the original decision, in general, through the permission to express the unsatisfied need;
- creation of the satisfaction of the need, or, as an alternative, becoming aware of the new options which the patient has;
- projection of the re-decision on the current situation (serves the patient in crystallising the result, acquiring the awareness of his own responsibility in the current situation);
- projection of the re-decision on the future, constructing a bridge for the time to come;
- liberating energy through the body.

Let us look at a case example.

The therapist, in a group (which is the chosen setting for the Gestalt re-decision techniques), establishes a contract with Giuliano:

T: "So, Giuliano, you want to work to be able to ask for what you need. OK. Now, I ask you to sit on that chair, and you will have before you that other empty chair. Agreed?"

[Work contract]

P: (Nods and sits.)

T: "I ask you to keep your eyes closed, breathe deeply . . . in the meantime, please, I ask everyone to remain in complete silence, to help Giuliano's concentration."

[First step]

T. "Now go into the episode that you told me about before with your girlfriend . . . you are in the scene . . . be yourself in that scene . . . describe in the present what you feel . . ."

[Second step]

P: "I am in front of Eleonora, I look at her . . . I like her, I feel full of heat . . . instinctively, I would like to kiss her . . ."

T: "What prevents you from doing it?"

[Confronts the patient's loss of power: "I would like to kiss her"]

P: "I am afraid that she does not want to . . . I would feel very bad . . ."

T: "Stay with this fear, and express it both with your voice and with a gesture . . ."

P: "I am afraid to kiss her, I am really afraid" [in a low voice, and stting rigidly in the chair with his arms crossed].

T: "Come on, say it louder, louder! And accompany it with a gesture of the hands!"

[Third step]

P: "I am afraid" [shouts and spreads out his arms, making a fist with his hands].

T: "Tell her what you are doing in your fear! Make your fists talk"

[contract with the script decision]

P: "I will keep you away, I will keep you away . . ." [he lowers his tone and starts to cry].

T: "With whom are you really talking?.

[Fourth step]

P: "I remember that it was like that with mum . . . it was the same . . ."

T: "Remain in the present . . . it is as if it were happening now . . . you have your mum in front of you . . ."

[Fifth step]

P: "[in tears] It is true, mum, I cannot kiss you . . . you are far away, you refuse me."

[Injunction: "Don't be intimate"]

T: "Tell your mother what you feel when she refuses you!"

[Sixth step]

P: "I hate you, I hate you! You always leave me alone!"

T: "You are very angry, you learnt to be afraid to ask mum, but it is she who is afraid of a kiss! Tell her that it is fair for you to be kissed!"

[Permission to express a need]

P: "Kiss me! Kiss me! I need you to kiss me . . . don't leave me!"

T: "Giuliano, it is beautiful to ask for a kiss, it is beautiful to kiss . . . you have protected yourself from the refusal of your mum by being afraid to ask, to avoid more refusals, but now you can decide that it is not frightening to ask, that it is mum who is afraid . . . and that is why she refuses you . . ."

[Seventh step]

P: "That's it, that's it . . . mum makes me angry when she refuses me, but I want to be kissed anyway . . . I will be kissed anyway . . . my aunt can kiss me . . . I will go to her!"

T: "Now leave mum and go back to Eleonora . . . tell her what you will do differently with her!"

[Eighth step]

P: "Eleonora, I love you, I like you, tonight I am with you, I want to be with you, and to kiss you, I know that you want it also . . ."

T: "Good, now make contact with the decision that you take, and imagine how your life will be in the future, giving yourself the permission to ask for what you need."

[Ninth step]

P: "It will be different . . . I will feel good with Eleonora, I will be satisfied, I will not be frightened that she does not love me . . . I can kiss her, she will also be happy, she can kiss me, she will not complain that I am cold . . ."

T: "You have done great work! Now conclude by expressing with your body how you feel!"

[Tenth step]

P: [Gets up, stretches himself, and, smiling, goes to hug a member of the group.]

In the second option, that of the intervention on the *rubberband*, one works in relation to an apparently neutral and banal stimulus, because of which the patient is "flung" from the *here-and-now* into an unexpected time and space, in an archaic experience, in a *there-and-then*.

As in the re-decisional intervention, here, too, the work to do is divided into steps:

- intensification of the emotions of racket manifested in the here-and-now;
- re-connection with the old scene;
- expression of need;
- awareness of the lack of satisfaction in that need;
- satisfaction of the need in the here-and-now and awareness of the new options;
- crystallisation of the re-decision;
- projection of the re-decision in the future.

Kupfer and Haimowitz (1970) suggested that the therapist facing a rubberband situation has four options:

- he can make a fantasy-hypothesis based on the child experience of the patient, to be verified subsequently with the patient himself: patient (to the therapist): "I feel sad because I am not well and you do not care about me . . ."; therapist: "When you were young, did you need to become ill in order to receive attention from your parents?"
- he can make a fantasy-hypothesis on the child experience of the patient and express it with an adult reaction. (Same situation as

previously.) Therapist: "You are behaving in a way that demands that I concentrate my attention on you, but without asking you directly what it is that you need";

- he can ignore the rubberband and remain in the here-and-now. Therapist: "I see that your expression has changed. What is happening?";

- he can alternate all three of the techniques described.

Both of the therapeutic options can be dealt with through the *two-chairs work*, conceived in the 1960s by Perls, to help people to appropriate different parts of the self. This technique entered into the practice of transactional analysis from Gestalt, being a very effective way to help the client to resolve archaic conflicts with the parents and other persons in the environment in which he was raised. In this technique, the therapist is only a guide and does not impersonate roles: the polarities are expressed and integrated by the patient with the direction of the therapist.

The therapist, after having established a *work contract* in which he explains the methods and desired end of the procedure, places an *empty chair* (projective seat) before the client, who is sitting on the so-called *hot seat*. He asks him to speak to someone or something (for example, a phobic object) connected to the problem; one can quickly understand that if someone or something is perceived as a parental figure, so that the client speaks from the Child ego state, when the therapist asks him to change places, occupying the chair that was empty before to express the other viewpoint, he usually gets a reply from the Parent ego state. In practice, there is an internal dialogue between the "warehouse" of parental information (as the person experienced the parental or other significant figures, *not* as those figures actually were) and the unsatisfied need and the decisions taken in relation to the lack of satisfaction of that need in the Child of the client.

McNeel (1976) maintains that, in the system of transactional analysis, what usually occurs during the two-chairs work consists of the dramatisation by the client of his states of Child–Parent ego, respectively, in the "hot seat" and in the "projective seat"; he emphasises, moreover, how one of the causes of failure of this type of intervention can consist of a vicious circle comprising a blocked confrontation between an Adapted Child who expects the other to change, and a Negative Normative Parent, or a "plastic" Negative Affective Parent.

For an effective application of the two-chairs work, the therapist should work according to some operative guidelines (Novellino, Eric Berne Institute Seminars):

- help the patient to *"feel like" that child*, turning to him as if he were; the same principle is valid when the patient, in the projective seat, enters into his own Parent, and then the therapist will communicate with that specific parental figure;
- ask the patient to remain in the present;
- ask the patient to talk *in the first person* and to have a dialogue with the counterpart, turning to him *directly* (I–you dialogue);
- pay attention to the *non-verbal messages* of the body to discern the emotion being exposed (respiration, look, muscular tone, unwitting gestures);
- help the patient to become aware and to *express the emotion*, amplifying it and translating it in simple words
- underline the *script beliefs and decisions* which emerge during the work.

Separation and condensation in the work of the two chairs

The type of indications that the therapist provides to the client about the moves to make on the two chairs assumes relevance in the direction of this type of work.

The client usually starts his work in the "hot seat", where he will energise his Child ego state, which he will turn to the imagined Parent in the "projective seat" (empty chair). In the course of the work, the therapist has the option of having the client move on to the "projective seat", and back again, therefore fostering a dialogue between the two parts in conflict. These moves risk being causal from a methodological point of view. A useful criterion for deciding whether to leave the client working on the "hot seat" or to have him impersonate the parent in the "projective seat" is based on the degree of impasses and on his defence mechanisms (Novellino, 1983).

The first step to take in methodological clarification in the two-chairs work is that of establishing the degree of the *impasses*, and, on this point, it is useful to consider the classification proposed by Woollams and Brown (1978) in two types of impasse, the first of the "I–you" type and the second of the "I–I" type. The first type includes the impasses of the first and second degree, while the second type corresponds to the impasse of the third degree.

Work on the two chairs according to the classification of Woollams and Brown

- I–You: impasse of the first and second type;
- I–I: impasse of the third type.

While the concepts explained by McNeel (1976) clarify the problems which emerge during the work of the two chairs having an impasse of the first type (I–You), to explain many cases of failure in the work of the two chairs applied to impasses of the second type (I–I), it can be useful to consider the defence mechanisms involved in the problem of the client.

We can, to this end, classify in two groups the defence mechanisms to consider in the environment of the two-chairs work.

1.   The first group, definable as *"separation"*, comprises defence mechanisms which give as a result the fact that the person expels his psychological content outside the limits of the personality membrane which encircle the three ego states. The defence mechanisms of projection (a clinical example in which this defence mechanism is active is given by the paranoid states) and of displacement (example, phobias) mainly appertain to this group. The two-chairs work of the A type, explained later (I–I), is applied to this group.

2.   The second group (definable as *"condensation"*), comprises defence mechanisms that have as a consequence the fact that the person keeps psychological content blocked inside the limits of the personality membrane, which are normally directed towards the external world. The defence mechanisms of introjection and of turning against the self (typical clinical example is depression) mainly appertain to this group. The two-chairs work of the B type (I–You) is applied to this group.

In *work of the A type*, the person dramatises in both the "hot seat" and the "projective seat", with the aim of his becoming aware of what appertains to the self, both with the part that he experiences as the "real self" and the part he expels outside (a phobic object, a persecution content, etc.): the patient elaborates an *I–I* relationship. The results are often dramatic in insight and cathartic effect. Usually, the work of the A type is indicated when a mechanism of separation is activated; keeping the client on the "hot seat", continuing to expel material against the "projective seat", often reinforces the separation itself.

Work of the B type consists of keeping the client in the "hot seat", helping him to direct the emotional charge, which he normally keeps directed against the self, towards the "projective seat", creating in this way an I–You relationship that persons who use mechanisms of condensation are extremely relutant to install. Having these persons move to the "projective seat", above all in the initial phase of the work, often reinforces their tendency to condensate.

A clinical case

The following material is taken from a supervision provided by a therapist in the interval between two therapy sessions, during which he worked with a very depressed forty-three-year-old client, in treatment for about a year.

First part (session preceding the supervision)

Client (C):   "Now I feel worse than usual, unappreciated . . ."

Therapist (T):   "Imagine your mother in front of you and tell her."

C: "Mum, I feel unappreciated."

T: "Now be your mother and reply" (the therapist follows the type A two-chairs work).

C: (after having moved to the projective chair) "Try, my daughter. Wasn't all the love I gave you enough?"

T: "Move to the other chair."

C: "It is true . . ." (becomes sadder).

The work lasts another ten minutes with the client, who moves to the other chair, elaborating the position of Victim in the hot seat.

During the supervision, it appears evident that, although it appears that the two-chairs work with the mother in the projective seat is coherent with the therapeutic plan being pursued with that client, the method followed by the therapist in directing the work was reinforcing the process of introjection of a "plastic" Parent, which the client endured passively (Victim), attributing the blame (but not the responsibility) for her state to herself. It was agreed, therefore, to try the two-chair method again, but keeping the client in the hot seat (type B).

Second part (session following the supervision)

C: "I feel exactly the same as the last time."

T: "Imagine again your mother in front of you and tell her."

C: "I feel unwell again."

T: "Tell her how you feel when you feel unwell."

C: "I feel sad, I tell myself that no one helps me and no one will help me."

T: (noting the tension of the jaws and of the throat): "You seem angry rather than sad . . ."

C: (surprised and confused) "It is not possible . . . I cannot be angry . . . with my mother."

T: "Tell her."

At this point, there follows work based on permission to express the anger. For the first time in a year, the patient stops looking at the floor when she speaks with others and looks into the eyes of the therapist while she talks to him. In the last part of the session, the client refers to "feeling alive" for the first time in many years, and agrees to pursue the work in that direction (which was then taken out of focus in a re-decisional work of ". . . forgive my mother, thank her for what she could do anyway, and go on my way").

When the therapy ended, the therapist identified in the last session the real starting point of a therapy which risked stagnating for a long time, and maybe even failing.

Take care though, because in patients with a regressive pre-Oedipal personality, which tends towards splitting, the technique of the chairs (two, three, five chairs, etc., according to Stuntz) *is contra-indicated,* as it encourages separation and splitting (here, the cohesive techniques, or tactics of the Self, are to be used as the initial Bernean operations).

In Table 6, I provide a summary of the principal characteristics of the work of the two chairs of type A and B.

Table 6. The two-chairs work.

Type A		Type B
3rd type	Impasse	1st and 2nd type
Separation	Defence mechanisms	Condensation
Dramatization	Projective chair	Empty
Phobias, paranoid states	Clinical use	Depression, psychosomatic illnesses
I–I	Externalised dialogue	I–You

Source: Novellino, 1983.

Another useful instrument of the two-chairs technique is the use of "heighteners" (McNeel, 1976), or short but full interventions, through which the therapist offers the patient new solutions and new interpretative modalities of the problem, putting emphasis on the more burdensome and self-limiting aspects of the patient himself, who, in this way, will be stimulated to energise other parts of his personality.

For example, for a person who, during the work in therapy, shows that he is waiting for his father to change, so as to be able to resolve the problems magically, appropriate "heighteners" could be:

"Tell your father that you will continue to be unwell until he decides to change . . .", or "Become aware that you are waiting to be able to be better. How long do you intend to continue with this?"

This situation, related to the magical expectation of changing someone else, is a rather recurrent theme in the two-chairs work, as is also the fact that the person, when he starts the dialogue, is most often in the position of Victim.

It is extremely important, for the therapy to be efficient, to identify, behind the real requests that the patient makes to the parental figure, the more profound psychological request, that is to say, that archaic request for satisfaction of a need that was not realised in the past, and which is often verbalised by using very simple and urgent words, such as *look at me, touch me, listen to me,* etc.

Rechilding

Clarkson and Fish (1988) propose a technique for a psychotherapy of the Child ego state. The aim is that of creating new states of the Child, starting from the premise that even the Child ego state is modified in the course of life. The technique calls for:

- a group setting of the workshop type;
- phases of decontamination, re-decision, and reparenting;
- regression to physiological phases with the guided creation of a new Child ego state;
- subsequent work of cognitive integration.

The meta-psychological support for the technique of Clarkson and Fish is provided by the theory of the dynamic Child (Blackstone, 1997): the latter takes issue with the Bernean thesis of the Child ego state as fixated in childhood, and hypothesises a Child who evolves during the whole cycle of life.

The three chairs technique

The three chairs technique (Kleeman, 1974) consists of guiding the patient, asking him to move towards a third chair, to evaluate from an *Adult perspective* the dialogue between his Parent and his Child, and, therefore, to come up with an answer, a solution, a compromise that can end the conflict in the area.

This answer can come from both the logical and rational parts of the Adult (in which case it will most probably be an option that tends towards compromise) and the intuitive part, that is, from the A1, and will assume in this case connotations of alternative solutions, creative ones "restructuring the field", in Gestalt terms.

Even though I have included it in this chapter on re-decisional techniques, the technique of the three chairs is more appropriately part of the strategic phase of *decontamination*.

Now let us see an example of clinical work with the three chairs.

Therapist (T): "Who wants to work?"

Patient (P): "I do!"

T: "Tell me what is the problem and how you want to feel and behave once you have solved it."

P: "I am afraid that one day my wife will leave me for someone else. I would like to feel calm and trust her."

T: "In what way has this problem presented itself to you in the past?"

P: "I have always thought that one shouldn't trust women too much."

The patient presents, from a structural point of view, a double contamination.

"One should not trust women" (contamination between Parent and Adult: the therapist is able to make a historical diagnosis as he has the information that the message comes both from the father and the grandfather).

"I am afraid because women can leave from one moment to the next" (contamination between Child and Adult: the diagnosis of the child ego state is derived from the information that when he was young, the patient often suffered separation from his mother due to her long work trips, and she also periodically abandoned the house after terrible fights with the father).

The therapist chooses to do a therapy of decontamination using the technique of the three chairs.

T: (after having explained the function of the three chairs) "Listen to what your Parent says about women."

P: (in the P chair) "Women . . . you never know what they are up to behind your back. Be careful with them!"

T: "Go to the chair of the Child and express your emotions."

P: (in the C chair) "I am afraid . . . if women are like that, I can never be happy."

T: "Go to the chair of the Adult and tell me what you think."

P: (smiling) "I think it is evident that I have been listening to the prejudices of my father since I was young . . ."

Subsequently, the therapist and the patient will have a conceptual base from which to explore the prejudices and the fears that have always prevented a spontaneous approach with the opposite sex.

Interventions on the Parent

In re-decisional literature, let us consider different works on the techniques applied directly to the Parent ego state of the patient. All of them, in essence, are united by two common elements:

- the first is that they are different from Berne's operations with the Parent, as these are interventions of the therapist that have the aim of supporting the Child to consent to a return to the operations on the Adult;
- the second is that they are fundamentally part of a re-decision process.

Let us consider them in synthesis.

The Parent interview

This is a useful technique, also used in the work with the two chairs (McNeel, 1976). The principal aim is to highlight the defensive position from which the real parent transmitted a script message. The patient realises that it derived from a parental phobia triggered by his legitimate and natural need and so can re-decide not to expect a change in the Parent, or to accept that it will never come. The theory behind this is the "Crazy Child in the Parent" (Holloway, 1974).

During this type of intervention, the therapist talks to the person seated in the projective chair as if she were effectively the parent *in person*.

In practice, this happens when the therapist, having recognised the position of Victim of the patient and his magical expectation of change, realises that the answers given during the dialogue of the parental projection are answers of defence, that is, to protect the state of the scared Child.

This technique is, therefore, useful in showing the patient, through stimulating his Little Professor, how the force, the impregnability, even the rudeness of the real parent, was, in reality, behaviour carried out to hide uneasiness and fear.

The therapist can start this type of intervention in the simplest way possible; for example, asking the parent his name, and continuing to ask questions about his feelings towards his son/daughter.

Initially, he will receive defensive answers, but if the interview is conducted in an effective way, sooner or later the defensive answers will diminish, maybe following questions of the type: "What do you feel when you see that your daughter wants to be stroked by you?"

In this way, an emotional reply will be elicited from the parental figure, who will then change his ego states, continuing from the Child (the Child in the Parent, in the second order structure). This change will encourage the patient to experience an *understanding of his parent that is different from his understanding of the actual parent*, as the part of the personality that is stimulated is the intuitive one of the A1.

McNeel recalls that the Parent Interview can be a very intense experience, so that in at least two types of cases, its application should be avoided.

The first concerns psychotic patients: an experience of that kind could cause very deep psychotic nuclei to explode, which would then be difficult to manage.

The second concerns those situations in which the therapist realises that the parental figure with whom the person is talking is seriously disturbed from a psychic point of view: for example, the figure of a mother who is "cold" and "ruthless". In this case, says McNeel, it is preferable not to lead the patient into the "hell" of another. To interrupt the Parent Interview, sometimes it is necessary for the therapist to leave, or to occupy the parental chair himself in order to take care of the scared Child directly.

Self-reparenting

This theory (James, 1974) deals with a therapeutic process that aims to restructure those negative parts of the Parent ego state that have transmitted script messages to the Child. Unlike the *reparenting* described by Schiff (1975), where the archaic Parent is excluded and replaced internally by a new Parent, incorporated in the psychotic patient through the global environment of the therapeutic community, in self-reparenting, it is the Adult of the patient that, guided by the therapist, establishes the strategies that will render automatic the new messages of self-reliance applied to the Free Child. Therefore, in essence, the patient learns the ways of self-parenting that help the Child to express the new needs of which he has become aware through Gestalt techniques. What distinguishes this technique from the others is that the new Parent derives from the Adult of the patient.

The Parent resolution process

This technique (Dashiell, 1978) is based on the assumption of a capacity of the Parent to formulate new permissions during the whole lifespan. A contract is drawn up between the Adult of the therapist and that of the patient, detailing the course of the therapy and the aim to pursue. The technique of the three chairs is used, through which a dialogue occurs between the therapist and the Parent of the patient, to whom the permissions that are lacking are provided.

Spot reparenting

This is also a technique aimed at restructuring the Parent in a deficient area (Osnes, 1974). The work is carried out in a regressive modality, helping the patient to return to a scene in which he experienced an unsatisfied need, and finding a positive message that permits the Child to feel authorised to express that need.

In-depth psychotherapy

Erskine (2003) proposed an in-depth psychotherapy for the Parent ego state, starting from the premise that the process of introjection lasts a whole lifetime.

Some of the above-mentioned techniques are compared in Moroney (1989).

Tactics of intervention on dreams

Berne (1961, 1966) talks of dreams as a metaphor expressed by the unconscious about the script:

> The therapist considers the patient's dream as a direct expression of the unconscious script protocol.

There is, in Bernean thought (1961) and in psychodynamic transactional analysis, a strong relation between:

> script (the old transference drama reproduced in the here-and-now);
> ⇩
> dream (the metaphor and sign of the script);
> ⇩
> dream (the clue of the transference).

The first dreams told, which can provide precious information about the expectations of the client and about the transference level of the therapeutic alliance that is under construction, are significant, relative to the psychodynamic meaning of the setting.

Some dreams can affirm positive signs of the *syndrome of effective psychotherapy* (emergence of new material); others indicate an evolution of transference.

In the transactional analysis literature, the following techniques are cited to "work" the dreams:

- *psychodramatic technique* (of Gestalt derivation);
- the five chairs technique of Stuntz (1973);
- interpretative technique.

Beyond the interpretative risks (or the projection by both the therapist and the patient), the two ways to arrive at the "personal meaning" of the dream are fundamentally those of:

- dramatising it, with a technique derived from Gestalt;
- analysing it, using the technique of free association, and interpreting it.

Both techniques are effective, but caution is to be used in confronting the work on dreams when one is treating a pre-Oedipal patient, remembering that the marginal pre-Oedipal patient (for example, *borderline*) shows an increased tendency for splitting in any regressive work, above all of a psychodramatic type.

The technique of Stunz is now only of historical interest. This consisted of dramatising the various parts of the dream, assigning the five chairs to them, corresponding to the five functions of the ego (NP, AP, A, AC, FC).

In applying the *Gestalt technique*, it is necessary first of all to avoid dramatising only one part, or only one symbolic aspect of the dream, because this way the global significance of it will evaporate. The therapist might recognise in a dream the symbolic nature of a scene that has great value to the script and decide that re-decisional work should be based on the oneiric plot. In this case, the therapist himself plays an active part, guiding the patient to explore the various parts of the dream, including those that would otherwise be neglected.

In the *interpretative technique*, the therapist will guide the patient towards *free associations* on the various components of the dream (Novellino, 1989, 1998):

> persons;
> places;
> objects, animals;
> actions.

The work starts from the exploration of possible recent events that might have caused the dream (day's residue). The aim will be to gather clinical material for a possible interpretation.

Let us take as a didactic example a dream brought by a patient, to illustrate how each of two tactics could be used: the first, interpretative, is that which is really carried out, the second, psychodramatic, is explained as a virtual option.

Enrico is a patient of about forty years of age, the director of a company, single, who requests a psychotherapy following a depressive reaction to a great disappointment in love.

He appears highly motivated, preferring not to take the psychopharmacological cure that was suggested by the neurologist who referred him. His psychotherapeutic contract concerns his intention to come out of the depression, finding enthusiasm again for new projects and for new love relationships, understanding the underlying reasons for his depressive reaction.

Enrico understands and accepts the various rules of the setting, which is based on two sessions a week.

About a month after the start of the therapy, he spontaneously relates a dream he had the previous night:

> "I found myself in my parents' house by the sea . . . where we went every summer, only that it seemed that I was the only one there, I don't see anyone else . . . I was in the living-room, that was exactly as it really was, the only difference was that there was a large bookcase, enormous, I tried to look at the books on the shelves, but I couldn't make out which books there were . . . at some point, I found myself in front of the sea, I knew how to swim, but I had a sort of reluctance to enter the water, the sea was calm, but it was as if it were warning of a sort of danger, and I remained there in front of the water, undecided . . . I woke up with this uneasiness . . ."

T: "Do you remember if you had any thoughts when you woke up while you felt this uneasiness?"

E: "I don't know ... yes, the fact that I wanted to remember it to talk about it here ..."

T: "OK. Can you think of anything that happened yesterday which could be tied to the dream in some way?"

[Day's residue]

E: "I had thought about it coming here—yes, maybe the fact that I was preparing some documents for the house where my mother lives now and that we have to sell ..."

T: "Continue to say what comes to mind ..."

[Free association]

E: "Well, it comes to mind that I did not tell my mother, actually no one, that I had started therapy ... I am ashamed in some way, I think I would appear weak, that I am not able to make it by myself ... that's it, maybe I think one thing from the dream ... those books come to mind which I am not able to read, to distinguish ..."

T: "In some way like a child who still does not know how to read ..."

E: "Sure ... true! ... in fact, now that you make me remember, I was like I am now, but it was as if I were young, because I remember that I was not able to reach the shelves of the bookcase ..."

T: "Listen, and what comes to mind at the sea?"

E: "I like it a lot, I went there always until some years ago ... in fact, I realise that it has been some years that for some reason or other I go little ... and in fact, I miss it ... I would like to return, I like being underwater a lot, to look at what is underneath ..."

T: "OK. I think that we have some useful elements for an explanation ... First, the central element is related to the experience of feeling like a young child at the beginning of the therapy; you are afraid of not being able to 'read' the books, or to understand what will come out from inside yourself during the therapy ... the bookcase in the family home probably represents the things of your childhood that are there written inside of you, but you are afraid of not reaching them, and of remaining alone in this task and not being able to do it, as you are afraid of remaining blocked in the face of this ..."

[Interpretation]

E: "You know what I am thinking . . . that in fact, after our last meeting, I left with the feeling of not being able to understand what you had said . . ."

[Confirms the interpretation]

T: "In a certain way, to read . . ."

E: "Exactly . . ."

The session continues with other considerations about how Enrico is experiencing the start of the therapy.

Now let us consider how the same dream could have been confronted with a Gestalt technique of psychodramatisation, distinguishing the principal steps:

- ask the patient to relate the dream in the present;
- have him explain the experiences, starting by impersonating the various parts of the dream (house, bookcase, sea, himself);
- dwell on the emotion that emerges, tying it to some scene from the script (for example, a sense of inadequacy or a childhood fear);
- direct towards a re-decisional technique.

Table 7 summarises a comparison between the two approaches.

Table 7. Summary of a comparison between the interpretative and the psychodramatic techniques.

Interpretive technique	Psychodramatic technique
Relate a dream	Relate a dream in the present
Look for the possible day's residue	Impersonate the various parts of the dream
Encourage free association	Encourage emotional contact
Link with relational events between patient and the therapist (transference)	Link with possible decisional scenes of the script
Interpretation	Re-decisional technique

CHAPTER NINE

The psychodynamic approach

Deconfusion in Berne

B erne wrote,

> The ultimate aim of transactional analysis is structural readjustment and reintegration. This requires first, restructuring, and secondly, reorganization ... Following the dynamic phase of reorganization, there is a secondary analytic phase which is an attempt to deconfuse the Child. (1961, p. 224)

He indicates *regression analysis* as an elective method that still remains at the prototype stage. In the case of Elise, a phobic patient, Berne (1966, p. 226) resorts to the individual treatment "on the couch". Again, in *Principles of Group Psychotherapy Treatment* (1966), he recalls that it is the task of the analyst to "decodify and disintoxicate" (p. 186) the old experiences of the Child, in the presence of the Adult of the therapist. To do this, he invokes the use of *interpretation*, but dis-sociating himself from the Freudian themes, strictly Oedipal, of the interpretation (p. 206) and recalling clearly, therefore, the concept of *re-decision*.

Deconfusion is the central phase in the Bernean methodology. To "deconfuse" literally means to "remove the confusion" of the Child ego state. For further theoretical study, refer to my works of 1998 and of 2004.

Hargaden and Sills (2003) have given an exhaustive definition of deconfusion, in line with Berne and with what I have written:

> Deconfusion is the process by which the therapist facilitates the patient to connect with her internal Child ego and bring experiences, feelings and sensations – in other words complex states of mind – into the therapeutic relationship. It is the process by which the patient is enabled to become more conscious. As the patient connects with her Child ego state, she will contact aspects of her self that as yet have remained under-developed (described as walled-off experiences and located in Co) . . . Through the process of the transferential relationship, this unconscious material will emerge in the relationship. The treatment plan involves the therapist's capacity and ability to be attentive, thoughtful and skilful in understanding her countertransferential responses. The methodology for deconfusion consists of an analysis of the domains of transference together with the therapist's use of emphatic transaction . . . The aim of deconfusion is the transformation of unconscious processes such as archaic, dormant and conflicted aspects of self, into a more conscious, vibrant and mature dynamic. (Hargaden & Sills, 2003, p. 188)

Deconfusion and re-decision

Deconfusion is a strategic phase that is, therefore, the moment in which to confront the decisions of the script so as to modify them, to *re-decide*. To deconfuse and to re-decide are concepts that can appear to be the same, but are operationally different:

We have already considered:

Deconfusion: strategic phase of resolution of the intrapsychic conflict; Re-decision: objective of the strategic phase.

- *Bernean deconfusion techniques* (interpretation and crystallisation);
- *post-Bernean deconfusion techniques* (the two-chairs technique, disconnecting rubberbands, rechilding of Clarkson and Fish, etc).

The *re-decision analysis of transference* is situated at the mid-point (Novellino, 1985b, 1987, 1998).

Strategic phase of deconfusion
⇩
- ● Bernean tactics: the two operations of crystallisation and interpretation.
- ● Redecision tactics:
- — redecision of the Gouldings;
- — disconnecting rubberbands of Erskine and Kupfer and Haimowitz;
- — interventions on the Parent;
- — rechilding (Clarkson & Fish).
- ● Psychodynamic tactics:
- — self-analysis of countertransference and re-decision analysis of transference (Novellino);
- — deconfusion of Hargaden and Sills.

Re-decision analysis of transference

Before passing to the concepts that are more precisely methodological, I consider it useful for the reader to complete the material of psycho-dynamic theory presented in Chapter Three, with the writings of Clarkson.

The latter (1992) devotes much space to the description of the different types of transference and countertransference, which I summarise in the following box:

- ● complementary transference (the patient tries to complement an interrupted symbolic relationship);
- ● concordant transference (the patient projects his own Child ego state in an attempt to establish an identification);
- ● destructive transference (the patient applies his old destructive fantasies to the therapist);
- ● facilitative transference (the patient transfers on to the therapist his own characteristics or style that was shown to be effective for him in the remote past).

The same author classifies in the following way the transference and countertransference events:

Transference and countertransference
Transference of the client (pro-active type).
Countertransference of the therapist (reactive type).
(Counter)transference of the therapist (pro-active type).
Countertransference of the client (reactive type).

According to Clarkson (1992), the countertransference events can therefore contain:

- the classic transference of the patient of script material on to the therapist: proactive transference;
- what the therapist brings to the relationship in reply to the material projected by the patient: reactive countertransference;
- what the therapist brings to the relationship of his own non-resolved experiences: proactive transference (or transference of the therapist);
- what the patient brings to the relationship in reply to the material projected by the therapist: countertransference of the patient.

From a clinical point of view, with the aim of a self-analysis of countertransference (Novellino, 1984a), the following processes are to be taken into account:

- if the therapist accepts, and if he hooks on to, the parental role projected by the patient, we have a *complementary identification* of the therapist. If the therapist activates the same ego states of the patient, there is *concordant identification*: for example, the patient is depressed and the therapist "feels down";
- in *alternating identification*, the patient projects one or the other pole of the internal dialogue between Parent and Child;
- *collusion*, which is a countertransference event of a symbiotic nature, corresponds to concordant identification: it is a twinned and mirrored contamination in which the dual experiences coincide. Being the result of a contamination, it remains outside the awareness of the Adult. The therapist feels a *racket emotion* analogous to that which the patient feels: interventions that are omitted, erroneous, or amplified are possible under this type of mirrored stimulus;
- the transactional analytic phenomenon that specifically recalls the transference–countertransference circularity is the *rubberband* (Kupfer & Haimowitz, 1970): in relation to an apparently neutral and banal stimulus, one or the other member of the therapeutic relationship emotionally returns to another space–time and to a script scene that reactivates script beliefs, fantasies, racket feelings connected to the scene, or to pure or visceral psychosomatic replies.

Having completed the theoretical baggage, we turn to some tactical instructions. *Useful questions* in foreseeing/analysing countertransference events that mine the operative field of each strategic phase, but that frequently can re-emerge in the emotional depths of the deconfusion phase, are:

- Who does this patient remind me of?
- Which of my unsatisfied needs do I attribute to him?
- Which ideal parental figure does he remind me of or I would like him to be?
- Who spoke like that?
- With whom did I have similar sensations or feelings?
- With whom did I behave in this way?
- What role does my script foresee for me in pursuing my profession?
- Which role does the patient impersonate in my script?
- Which role do I impersonate in the patient's script?

To complete the description of the technical modalities to apply to transactional analysis according to a psychodynamic approach, let us consider in greater detail the *re-decision analysis of transference* (Novellino, 1985b, 1987, 1998).

This calls for:

- the operations of Bernean confrontation and explanation in the presence of a transaction of transference;
- an explanation on the psychodynamic level of the transaction (analysis of the projection);
- an interpretation of the protocol origin of the projection.

In parallel, in order to confront the unconscious dynamics in the therapeutic relationship, the following are considered structural:

- the analysis of countertransference;
- the analysis of unconscious contamination;
- the analysis of dreams.

In the individual setting, the use of the *couch* is taken up again in selected cases, the aim of which is to be explained and agreed upon with the patient in the first meetings.

It should be explained to the patient that, through *relaxation* and the *suspension of the face to face* method, the contact with the Child ego state is favoured: memories, free association, fantasies, physical sensations, and emotional states are better gathered in that way than in the frontal position.

I shall illustrate with a clinical example the three above-mentioned phases.

Eliana is a patient of about forty years of age, in psychotherapy for about two years, back from other attempts at psychotherapy, all interrupted because of intense unresolved transference phenomena: in the case of a female therapist, Eliana suffered from a strong sense of envy and jealousy, in the case of a male therapist, a chaotic erotic transference developed. The initial contract was about her incapacity to develop emotional relationships and about the objective to be able to be open and have genuine intimacy with the opposite sex. The patient had lived from the age of twenty to thirty-five in a religious community, which she had left and renounced her vows. The whole first phase of therapeutic work was devoted to the analysis of her contaminations and her psychological games. The central contaminations were about parental messages of a sexophobic type ("Men are animals" from the mother, and "You are not a real woman" from the father); the principal psychological game was "Rapo". Eliana had fought all her life to mediate between her affective and sexual drives, and the parent injunctions of "don't be a woman" and "don't be intimate with men"; her religious culture had reinforced her script apparatus. When she begins to understand the nature of her conflict, she starts a depressive phase, to which she reacts by developing feelings of intense attachment to the therapist, after an initial phase of rational detachment, justified also by the previous unhappy therapeutic experiences. She comes to a session with a parcel, and asks the therapist to accept it and to open it, but only after the session. The therapist comments:

> "I think instead we should discuss your request . . . ." [confrontation].
>
> "But why do you treat me in such a rigid way?" [transference transaction from Child to Parent].
>
> "What do you feel towards me at this moment?" [transaction of permission].
>
> (She remains silent, tense.)
>
> "I feel not understood . . . angry . . . maybe rejected . . ." [rubberband].
>
> [The therapist enters into contact with the countertransference: he tries, in turn, to feel attached and to attempt to reject the patient, through the

fantasy of sending her away. In a quick and intuitive self-analysis, he understands that he is feeling something similar to the patient [concordant identification] and that he is identifying with one rejecting part of the patient [complementary identification].

"When was it that you felt something similar?" [interrogation].

"... it was when I waited for a long time for my father to return ... he was never there ... then when he was there, he was immediately occupied by arguing with my mother. My sister and I went into a corner and waited until it was finished ..."

[At this point, the therapist would have the option of following the re-decisional route, for example, by disconnecting the rubberband, but chooses to follow the re-decision analysis of the transference, counting on the capacity that the patient has to relive her emotions connected with the unresolved dynamic with the father that she has projected on to him.]

"Maybe in those moments you hoped for ... dreamed of something different?" [interrogation that prepares an interpretation].

"I am not sure, but I think that I imagined that when Dad was alone, I could finally be close to him, alone, and I could have ... enjoyed it a little, not angry, not distracted ..." (her eyes fill with tears).

"I think it is very important that you are able to put yourself in contact with this emotion ... [intervention of support with the Parent] ... do you agree that we should see together what is happening?"

(The patient nods.)

"We will return soon to this emotion; for now we can talk of your request to give me a parcel and that I open it by myself. Let's say that offering me a parcel and asking me to see its contents outside the session was a sort of request for complicity ... do you agree?"

(Nods.)

"So, a transaction that comes from your Child part. OK? [Operation of explanation.] According to you, to which part of mine was your request directed?"

"Maybe to your child part ..."

"OK, I think it is true ... you talked about your fantasy of your father being alone with you ... so I would say that it is as if you had fantasised about finding the Child part of your father, to be close to him, to rescue him from the oppressive relationship with your mother" [operation of interpretation].

(Eliana nods, breathes deeply.)

"Are you ready for something else?"

(Nods.)

"I think that you, as a child, constructed a world in which sooner or later you would have had your father all to yourself, and that is understandable, given his absence. You experienced our sessions, carried out 'by adults', as excluding the emotional type of demands. I have become a distant emotional father, so to get close in a different way, far from the rationality of the session, you bring a gift in order to satisfy the need to create a parallel situation of fantasy; to experience with me the fantasy of a father rescued from the reality. Listen, what do you want to do with this parcel?"

"It is hard for me, I am telling you the truth ... but I understand that for my therapy it is right that you open it now ... in reality, it is only a letter ..."

"So it is a message ... [operation of specification] I think it is the right decision ... For you it is an opportunity to live in reality instead of in fantasy!" [Permission.]

What has happened is that Eliana has started to go back to her script modality, which had always caused her to experience impossible relationships, to suffer disappointments. The work on her transference will permit her to experiment, in a protected environment, with the fantasies and emotions that had led her into psychological games, even dramatic ones, and that, above all, had reinforced her conviction that reality would never have let her have a real relationship with a man.

In conclusion, let us explore the analysis of a dream.

Roberto is a man of about fifty who requests psychotherapy for a state of decision-making conflict; on the one hand, he is unable to decide to leave his wife, whom he married thirty years ago and with whom he has two children; on the other hand, he is unable to start a new life with a woman he has loved for three years. He has a phobic–obsessive structure, dependent personality traits, a "never" script (I will "never" have the love I want), plays games of "psychiatry", reinforced by a previous lengthy orthodox analysis. His contract is about "taking a decision within six months" and "expressing emotions instead of living only with the mind". The setting calls for a weekly session and the use of the couch.

After ten sessions, he relates the following dream:

"I am in my car, unexpectedly the radiator bursts, boiling water comes into the passenger compartment, entering through the dashboard, I, instead of doing something about the motor, I start drying, on my knees, then I think that the others see me and criticise me because I only take care of the details . . . well, yes, I am myself, I really lose myself in details . . . but I don't know what it means . . . but I was not anxious, in fact, I was happy, amused . . ."

"Do you remember if there was some episode which could be tied to this?"

[Day's residue]

(Long silence) ". . . yes, during the day I had had a discussion with my son . . . I wanted him to come with me on a trip . . . he had said yes, then on the telephone, when I asked him for confirmation, he remained silent. I felt blocked, I didn't know what to say to him, so I told him to think about it and that we would talk again . . ."

"And what is the link for you?"

"I think it is evident, I was not able to speak, I was blocked . . . in such cases I become blocked, I don't know what I feel, and the words do not come to me . . ."

"What makes you think of the radiator?"

[Free associations]

"I don't know . . . maybe the fact . . . a radiator cools the liquid . . . it makes me think of my block, that is, everyone tells me that I am a little cold . . . in fact, after the phone call, I was at home and I started to look at some cases from work . . . could it be?"

"In fact, it could be, in the sense that the car would represent your ego, your conscious personality, that you fear will be invaded by intense emotions, and you defend yourself with the things you have to do, thinking of practical things, even with your son you ended the conversation as 'between adults', asking your son to think about it and decide . . . we saw in the first interviews that this was the way in which you as a child defended yourself during the terrible fights which would suddenly erupt between your father and your mother . . ."

[Interpretation]

(He remains silent for a while.) "Really I remember this, it was difficult for me to contain my anger, I would have liked to kill my father, it was his fault . . ."

[Confirmation of the interpretation.]

In the following sessions, work with the two chairs is also under-taken, to help Roberto to come into contact with, and to express, his emotions, and, thus, to avoid the risk of transforming his awareness into a new game of intellectualisation ("psychiatry").

Deconfusion in a relational prospective

According to Hargaden and Sills (2003), the task of the therapist in the deconfusion is twofold:

- to be available to contain the non-integrated projective experi-ences expressed in the transference relationship
- to answer in an appropriate way to the unsatisfied relational needs coming from the child of the patient.

This twofold task calls for *four steps*, interrelated between them.

Development of an empathic relationship

This phase is based on use of the *empathic transaction* (Clark, 1991), seen as a type of ulterior transaction, in which the social level occurs between the Adult ego state of the patient and the therapist, while the psychological level is carried out between the Child ego state of the patient and the Adult ego state of the therapist: "An emphatic transaction occurs when the therapist communicates his or her under-standing of what the patient is experiencing and the patient experi-ences being understood" (Clark, 1991, p. 93).

Management of the transference relationship

Hargaden and Sills (2001) consider the transference "as the vehicle by which the therapist finds out the unconscious aspects of the patient" (p. 61).

The transference relationship becomes central to the comprehen-sion of the unconscious. Three types of transference are distinguished:

- *projective transference*: consists of the projection on to the therapist of objects "good" and "bad" (P1+ and P1−), has a defensive aim, and references the work of Moiso (1985);

- *introjective transference*: the patient tries to enter into symbiosis with the therapist to satisfy his evolutionary needs;
- *transformative transference*: occurs through the mechanism of projective identification.

The examination of countertransference

For an explanation of this phase, please refer to the work on the self-analysis of countertransference (Novellino, 1984).

Answering the patient with the use of empathetic interventions

On the whole, the importance of returning to Bernean therapeutic operations in an empathetic sense should be underlined.

GLOSSARY

A1: Little Professor.

A2: Adult in the second order structural analysis.

AC: Adapted child.

Acting out: Action of unloading non-thought-out emotions, both in transference and in countertransference.

Adult: State of the neopsychic ego that processes the relation of the ego with the here-and-now in a way which is free from exteropsychic and archeopsychic influences.

Alliance: Strategic initial phase of the psychotherapy, which calls for establishing a therapeutic contract, parallel to a positive transference and countertransference.

Analysis: Includes the two processes of reconstructive psychotherapy and of didactic analysis, both based on contracts of self-reliance.

Anti-leadership alpha: Process of rebellion explicit to the leader of the group.

Anti-leadership beta: Process of rebellion implicit to the leader of the group.

Ao: Adult in the third order structural analysis.

AP: Affective Parent.

C1: Somatic Child.

C2: Child in the second order structural analysis.

Child: State of the archeopsychic ego which processes the here-and-now based on childish functions.

Co: Child in the third order structural analysis.

Constructive transactional analysis: Application of constructive cognitivism to transactional analysis.

Contract: Agreement between patient and therapist on the ways and the how-tos of the therapy.

Counter-resistance: System of defence derived from a negative counter-transference.

Countertransference: All of the experiences of the therapist with regard to the patient.

Deconfusion. Strategic phase aimed at the resolution of the impasses.
   − *relational.* Approach of Hargaden and Sills.

Decontamination: Strategic phase aimed to the recovery of the executive power by the Adult.

Defence: Unconscious mechanism of the ego aimed at protecting from unacceptable unconscious experiences.

Didactic analysis: Psychotherapy applied to psychotherapists in training.

Ego state: Intrapsychic system, coherent in thought, emotions, and programmes of behaviour

Egogram: Diagram of energetic distribution between the five functions of the ego.

FC: Free Child.

Fourth rule: Rule of communication applied to unconscious communication.

Identification:
   − *alternating.* Unconscious mechanism in which the projection of a Parental pole and of a Child pole alternates on the therapist.
   − *complementary.* Unconscious mechanism in which the therapist identifies with the Parent which the patient projects on to him.
   − *concordant.* Unconscious mechanism in which the therapist identifies with the Child which the patient projects on to him.

Impasse: Goulding's theory of intrapsychic conflict, which describes three types of blocks between Parent and Child.
   − *affective.* Describes the second type of impasse in transference terms.
   − *cognitive.* Describes the first type of impasse in transference terms.
   − *somatic.* Describes the third type of impasse in transference terms.
   − *transference.* Applies the theory of impasses to transference relationships.

Internal dialogue: Intrapsychic transaction between Parent and Child.
   − *sequence of four internal dialogues* described by Kahler.

Method:
- *clinical*. Theory of psychotherapy based on the study of the relational events which distinguish the therapeutic interaction.
- *experimental*. Application of the principle scientific methods to psychotherapy.

Methodology: Theory of the technique.

Narrativism: Epistemological tendency applied to psychotherapy.

NP: Normative Parent.

Observing ego: Adult ego state capable of self-observing the clinical intrapsychic dynamics; aim of the decontamination.

OK-ness: Philosophical principle that ascertains that any human being is born with a positive potential towards life.

Operations: Therapeutic technique in a Bernean sense.

P1: Electrode.

P2: Parent in the second order structural analysis.

Parent: State of the exteropsychic ego that processes the here-and-now based on introjected models.

Persecutor: Dramatic role expressed by the negative NP.

Po: Parent in the third order structural analysis.

Pseudo-alliance: Dynamic relationship between the therapist and the patient based on its dramatic roles.

Psychodynamic approach: Roman school of Novellino and Moiso.

Psychological game: Dynamic relationship constructed on psychological roles that lead to a predetermined outcome.

Psychotherapy
- *focal*. Based on a contract of social control (= reparative).
- *integrative*. School of transactional analysis of Erskine.
- *reconstructive*. Based on a contract of autonomy.
- *re-decisonal*. School of transactional analysis of Goulding.
- *reparative* = Focal.

Racket: Intrapsychic and relational process that confirms the script.

Rechilding: Technique of deconfusion of Clarkson.

Re-decision: Objective of the strategic phase of the deconfusion.

Re-decision of transference: Process of deconfusion based on the self-analysis of countertransference and on the application of the Bernean operations to the analysis of transference (Novellino).

Relational transactional analysis: School of Hargaden and Sills.

Relearning: Strategic phase of concluding the therapy.

Rescuer: Dramatic role expressed by the negative AP.

Resistance: Block of the therapeutic process in consequence to defence mechanisms.
- *triadic*. Individual, cultural, and environmental system of defence.

Rules of communication: Three rules of Berne relative to the three types of transactions.

School of transactional analysis: Didactic and research groups recognised internationally.

Script decision: Self-limiting choice of survival taken in the first years of life.

Script matrix: Graphic outline that describes the diverse script messages transmitted from two parents to the child.

Sloppiness: Physiological unpredictability in the therapeutic relationship.

Strategy: Focal phase of the methodology.

Syndrome of effective psychotherapy: All of the positive results of the application of the experimental method.

Tactic: Technique specific to reach a strategic objective.

Therapeutic plan: Application of the methodology to a clinical case.

Transactional psychoanalysis: Application of the psychodynamic approach to the individual setting.

Transactions: Exchange of stimuli between the ego states of two or more participants.
- *bilogical*. Expressions parallel to primary and secondary processes.
- *empathic*. Ulterior transaction with which the therapist manifests to the patient his understanding of his experiences.
- *of countertransference*. Reply with the parent of the therapist to the Adult of the patient.
- *of transference*. Reply with the Child of the patient to the Adult of the therapist.
- *monologic*. Expression of only the secondary process.

Transference: All of the experiences by the patient towards the therapist as a substitute parental figure.

Unconscious communication: Series of transactions based on a symbolic narration that describes experiences regarding the therapist.

Victim: Dramatic role acted by the AC.

REFERENCES

Allen, J. R., & Allen, B. A. (2000). Every revolution should have dancing: biology, community organization, constructivism and joy. *Transactional Analysis Journal, 30*: 188–192.

Allen, J. R., & Allen, B. A. (2005). On receiving the 1988 Eric Berne Memorial Award for theory. *Transactional Analysis Journal, 29*(1): 11–13.

Barnes, G. (Ed.) (1977). *Transactional Analysis After Eric Berne.* New York: Harper's College Press.

Berne, E. (1961). *Transactional Analysis in Psychotherapy. A Systematic Individual and Social Psychiatry.* New York: Grove Press.

Berne, E. (1962). In treatment. *Transactional Analysis Bulletin, 1*(2): 10.

Berne, E. (1964). *Games People Play.* New York: Grove Press.

Berne, E. (1966). *Principles of Group Treatment.* New York: Grove Press.

Berne, E. (1972). *What Do You Say After You Say Hello?* New York: Grove Press.

Berne, E. (1977). *Intuition and Ego States.* San Francisco, CA: T. A. Press.

Blackstone, P. (1997). The dynamic child: integration of second-order structure, object-relations, and self psychology. *Transactional Analysis Journal, 27*(1): 216–234.

Boyd, L. (1986). Closing escape hatches. *Transactional Analysis Journal, 16*(4): 247–248.

Campos, L. P. (2003). Care and maintainance of the tree of transactional analysis. *Transactional Analysis Journal, 332*: 115–125.

Casalegno, P. (2005). La conclusione come fase strategica della terapia [The conclusion as a strategic phase of psychotherapy]. *Giornate AIAT*, Torino: 12–13 March.

Clark, B. D. (1991). Emphatic transaction in the deconfusion of the child ego state. *Transactional Analysis Journal, 21*(2): 92–98.

Clarkson, P. (1992). *Transactional Analysis Psychotherapy: An Integrated Approach*. London: Tavistock/Routledge.

Clarkson, P., & Fish, S. (1988). Rechilding: creating a new past in the present as a support for the future. *Transactional Analysis Journal, 18*(1): 51–59.

Cornell, W. F. (1986). Setting the therapeutic stage: the initial sessions. *Transactional Analysis Journal, 16*(1): 4–10.

Crossman, P. (1966). Permission and protection. *Transactional Analysis Bulletin, 5*(19): 152–154.

Dashiell, S. R. (1978). The parent resolution process: reprogramming psychic incorporations in the parent. *Transactional Analysis Journal, 8*(4): 289–294.

Drye, R. (1974). Stroking the rebellious child. *Transactional Analysis Journal, 4*(3): 289–294.

English, F. (1975). The three-cornered contract. *Transactional Analysis Journal, 5*: 383–384.

Erskine, R. G. (1974). Therapeutic interventions: disconnecting rubber-bands. *Transactional Analysis Journal, 4*(1): 7–8.

Erskine, R. G. (1980). Script cure: behavioral, intrapsychic and physiological. *Transactional Analysis Journal, 10*(2): 102–106.

Erskine, R. G. (2003). Introjection, psychic presence and Parent ego state: considerations for psychotherapy. In: H. Hargaden & C. Sills (Eds.), *Ego States* (pp. 83–108). London: Worth.

Erskine, R. G., & Moursund, J. P. (1988). *Integrative Psychotherapy in Action*. Newbury Park, CA: Sage.

Erskine, R. G., & Trautmann, R. (1996). Methods of an integrative psychotherapy. *Transactional Analysis Journal, 26*(4): 316–328.

Gilbert, M. (2003). Ego states and ego state network: some questions for the practitioner. In: H. Hargaden & C. Sills (Eds.), *Ego States* (pp. 232–246). London: Worth.

Gildebrand, K. (2003). An introduction to the brain and the early development of the Child ego state. In: H. Hargaden & C. Sills (Eds.), *Ego States* (pp. 1–27). London: Worth.

Goulding, R. (1972). New directions in transactional analysis: creating an environment for redecision and change. In: C. J. Sager & H. S. Kaplan (Eds.), *Progress in Group and Family Therapy* (pp. 105–134). New York: Brunner/Mazel.

Goulding, R., & Goulding, M. (1976). Injunction, decision and redecision. *Transactional Analysis Journal*, 6(1): 41–48.

Goulding, R., & Goulding, M. (1978). *The Power is in The Patient*. San Francisco, CA: TA Press.

Goulding, R., & Goulding, M. (1979). *Changing Lives Through Redecision Therapy*. New York: Brunner/Mazel.

Hargaden, H., & Sills, C. (2001). Deconfusion of the child ego state: a relational perspective. *Transacional Analysis Journal*, 31(1): 55–70.

Hargaden, H., & Sills, C. (Eds.) (2003). *Ego States*. London: Worth.

Harris, T. A. (1971). *I'm OK, You're OK*. New York: Grove Press.

Haykin, M. D. (1980). Type casting: the influence of early childhood experience upon the structure of the ego state. *Transactional Analysis Journal*, 10(4): 354–364.

Holloway, W. H. (1974). *Shut the Escape Hatch. The Monograph Series, IV*. Medina, OH: Midwest Institute for Human Understanding.

James, M. (1974). Self reparenting: theory and process. *Transactional Analysis Journal*, 4(3): 32–39.

James, M. (Ed.) (1977). *Techniques in Transactional Analysis*. Menlo Park, CA: Addison-Wesley.

Kahler, T. (1978). *Transactional Analysis Revisited*. Little Rock, AK: Human Development Publications.

Kleeman, J. (1974). The case of three chairs. *Transactional Analysis Journal*, 4(2): 29–30.

Kupfer, D., & Haimowitz, M. (1970). Rubberbands now, Part I. *Transactional Analysis Journal*, 1(2): 1–16.

Langs, R. (1988). *A Primer of Psychotherapy*. New York: Gardner Press.

Lee, A. (2003). The mirror exercise: creating new ego states now – a constructivistic approach. In: H. Hargaden & C. Sills (Eds.), *Ego States* (pp. 73–82). London: Worth.

McNeel, J. (1976). The parent interview. *Transactional Analysis Journal*, 6: 61–68.

McNeel, J. (1977). The seven components of redecision therapy. In: G. Barnes (Ed.), *Transactional Analysis After Berne* (pp. 425–441). New York: Harper's College Press.

Mellor, K. (1980). Impasses. *Transactional Analysis Journal*, 10(3): 213–220.

Mitchell, S. A. (1988). *Relational Concepts in Psychoanalysis. An Integration.* Cambridge, MA: Harvard University Press.

Moiso, C. (1985). Ego states and transference. *Transactional Analysis Journal, 15*(3): 194–201.

Moiso, C., & Novellino, M. (1982). *Stati dell'Io. Le basi teoriche dell'Analisi Transazionale Integrata* [Ego States. The Theoretical Basis of Integrative Transactional Analysis]. Rome: Astrolabio.

Moroney, M. K. (1989). Reparenting strategies in transactional analysis therapy: a comparison of five methods. *Transactional Analysis Journal, 19*(1): 35–41.

Novellino, M. (1983). Separazione e condensazione nel lavoro delle due sedie [Separation and condensation in the two-chair work]. *Neopsiche, 1*(2): 28–30.

Novellino, M. (1984a). Self-analysis of countertransference in integrative TA. *Transactional Analysis Journal, 14*(1): 63–67.

Novellino, M. (1984b). The effective psychotherapy syndrome: the experimental method applied to psychotherapy with TA. *Transactional Analysis Journal, 14*(2): 120–123.

Novellino, M. (1985a). Antileadership in TA groups. *Transactional Analysis Journal, 15*(2): 164–167.

Novellino, M. (1985b). Redecision analysis of transference: a TA approach to transference neurosis. *Transactional Analysis Journal, 15*(3): 202–206.

Novellino, M. (1987). Redecision analysis of transference: the unconscious dimension. *Transactional Analysis Journal, 17*(1): 27; 14(1): 63–67; 1–276.

Novellino, M. (1989). Il sogno nell' analisi transazionale clinica [The dream in transactional analysis]. *Quaderni dell' IAT*, Napoli: Marotta.

Novellino, M. (1990). *Conflitto intrapsichico e ridecisione* [Intrapsychic Conflict and Redecision]. Rome: Città Nuova.

Novellino, M. (1991). *Psicologia clinica dell'Io* [Clinical Psychology of the Ego]. Rome: Astrolabio.

Novellino, M. (1998). *L'approccio clinico dell'analisi transazionale* [The Clinical Approach to Transactional Analysis]. Milan: Franco Angeli.

Novellino, M. (2002). Psicoanalisi transazionale: una nuova tassonomia delle transazioni di transfert [Tansactional psychoanalysis: a new taxonomy of transference transactions]. *Atti del Convegno SIAT*, Rome, 11–13 October.

Novellino, M. (2003a). Transactional psychoanalysis. *Transactional Analysis Journal, 33*(3): 223–230.

Novellino, M. (2003b). On closer analysis: a psychodynamic review of the rules of communication within the framework of transactional psychoanalysis. In: H. Hargaden & C. Sills (Eds.), *Key Concepts in Transactional Analysis: Vol. I, Ego States* (pp. 149–168). London: Worth.

Novellino, M. (2004). *Psicoanalisi transazionale* [Transactional Psychoanalysis]. Milan: Franco Angeli.

Novellino, M. (2005). Transactional psychoanalysis: the epistemological foundations. *Transactional Analysis Journal*, 35(2): 157–172.

Novellino, M. (2008). Sloppiness e psicoanalisi transazionale [Sloppiness and transactional psychoanalysis]. *Atti del Convegno IAT-AIAT*, Turin, 7 December 2008.

Novellino, M. (2010). Il setting individuale in psicoanalisi transazionale [Individual setting in transactional psychoanalysis]. *3°EATA Colloquium*, Florence, 6 Maggio, 2010.

O'Leary, W. M. (1969). It's too soon to terminate. *Transactional Analysis Bulletin*, 8(29): 3–4.

Osnes, R. (1974). Spot-reparenting. *Transactional Analysis Journal*, 4(3): 40–46.

Schiff, J. L. (1975). *Cathexis Reader*. New York: Harper & Row.

Semi, A. (1988). *Trattato di psicoanalisi* [*Textbook of Psychoanalysis*]. Milan: Raffaello Cortina ed.

Shmukler, D. (2003). Ego states: a personal reflection. In: H. Hargaden & C. Sills (Eds.), *Key Concepts in Transactional Analysis* (pp. 135–148). London: Worth.

Steiner, C. M. (1974). *Script People Live*. New York: Grove Press.

Steiner, C., & Novellino, M. (2005). Theoretical diversity: a debate about transactional analysis and psychoanalysis. *Transactional Analysis Journal*, 35(2): 110–118.

Stern, D. (2005). Intersubjectivity. In: E. S. Pearson, A. M. Cooper, & G. O. Gabbard (Eds.), *The American Psychiatric Publishing Textbook of Psychoanalysis* (pp. 77–92). Washington, DC: American Psychiatric Publishing.

Stewart, J. (1992). *Eric Berne*. London: Sage.

Stuntz, E. (1973). Multiple chairs technique. *Transactional Analysis Journal*, 3(2): 105–108.

Tudor, K. (2002). Transactional analysis supervision or supervision analyzed transactionally? *Transactional Analysis Journal*, 32(1): 39–55.

Tudor, K. (2003). The neopsyche: the integrating Adult ego state. In: H. Hargaden & C. Sills (Eds.), *Ego States* (pp. 201–231). London: Worth.

White, R. B., & Gilliland, R. M. (1975). *Elements of Psychopathology. The Mechanisms of Defense*. New York: Grune and Stratton.

Woods, K., and Woods, M. (1999). Fascination as a result of conscious and unconscious ego states. *Transactional Analysis Journal, 19*(2): 80–85.

Woollams, S., & Brown, M. (1978). *Transactional Analysis.* Dexter, MI: Huron Valley Institute Press.

INDEX

For Product Safety Concerns and Information please contact our EU
representative GPSR@taylorandfrancis.com
Taylor & Francis Verlag GmbH, Kaufingerstraße 24, 80331 München, Germany